# YOUR recipe could appear in our next cookbook!

Share your tried & true family favorites with us instantly at
## www.gooseberrypatch.com
If you'd rather jot 'em down by hand, just mail this form to...
Gooseberry Patch • Cookbooks – Call for Recipes
PO Box 812 • Columbus, OH 43216-0812

### If your recipe is selected for a book, you'll receive a FREE copy!

*Please share only your original recipes or those that you have made your own over the years.*

Recipe Name:

Number of Servings:

Any fond memories about this recipe? Special touches you like to add or handy shortcuts?

Ingredients (include specific measurements):

Instructions (continue on back if needed):

Special Code: **cookbookspage**

*Over*

*Extra space for recipe if needed:*

## Tell us about yourself...

Your complete contact information is needed so that we can send you your FREE cookbook, if your recipe is published. Phone numbers and email addresses are kept private and will only be used if we have questions about your recipe.

Name:

Address:

City:                              State:              Zip:

Email:

Daytime Phone:

Thank you!  Vickie & Jo Ann

# Grandma's Best
# Christmas
## RECIPES

Treasured family recipes
for every holiday occasion.

## Gooseberry Patch

### An imprint of Globe Pequot
64 South Main Street
Essex, CT 06426

# www.gooseberrypatch.com

## 1•800•854•6673

Copyright 2024, Gooseberry Patch  978-1-62093-576-7

## Do you have a tried & true recipe...

tip, craft or memory that you'd like to see featured in a **Gooseberry Patch** cookbook? Visit our website at **www.gooseberrypatch.com** and follow the easy steps to submit your favorite family recipe. Or send them to us at:

Gooseberry Patch
PO Box 812
Columbus, OH 43216-0812

Don't forget to include the number of servings your recipe makes, plus your name, address, phone number and email address. If we select your recipe, your name will appear right along with it... and you'll receive a **FREE** copy of the book!

# Contents

# Dedication

*To everyone who loves homemade sugar cookies, packages wrapped in pretty papers, twinkling lights on the tree, an old-fashioned Christmas at Grandma's house...and sharing it all with family.*

# Appreciation

*To our family & friends...thank you for sharing your most cherished recipes and sweetest memories with us.*

# Waking Up
# at
# Grandma's

# Grandma's Best *Christmas* RECIPES

## Momma's Christmas Morning Casserole

*Jacki Smith*
*Fayetteville, NC*

*Every Christmas Eve, Momma would put together this casserole. Then on Christmas morning, she would pop it in the oven along with some orange danishes, and serve it for breakfast after presents were opened. I continue this tradition with my own family. It's wonderful with sweet pastries and fresh fruit.*

6 slices bread, crusts trimmed
softened butter to taste
mustard to taste
1 lb. ground pork sausage
8 eggs, beaten

1-1/2 c. milk
salt and pepper to taste
8-oz. pkg. shredded Cheddar
  cheese

Spread bread slices on one side with butter and mustard. Arrange butter-side up in a lightly greased 13"x9" baking pan; set aside. Brown sausage in a skillet over medium heat; drain. Spread sausage over bread slices. In a separate bowl, whisk together eggs, milk and seasonings; spoon over sausage layer. Sprinkle with Cheddar cheese; cover and refrigerate overnight. The next morning, uncover; bake at 325 degrees for 45 minutes, or until golden. Makes 10 servings.

It's Christmastime...a vintage Santa mug at every place setting is sure to put everyone in a holiday mood!

# Waking Up at Grandma's

## Traditional Banket

*Lauren Phillips*
*Grandville, MI*

*Banket is a traditional Dutch breakfast pastry. My grandma made it every year for Christmas. She'd also make it for my dad and myself as our birthday treat. The recipe has has been passed down from my great-great grandma. After my grandma passed away, I searched through her recipe cards until I found the recipe. Now it can continue to be passed down!*

4 c. all-purpose flour
1 lb. butter, softened
1 c. cold water
1 c. almond paste, shredded

3 eggs, beaten
2 c. sugar
Garnish: additional flour,
    beaten egg, sugar

Add flour to a large bowl; cut in butter until mixture forms crumbs. Stir in cold water until a dough forms; cover and refrigerate overnight. For filling, combine almond paste, eggs and sugar in another bowl; mix well. Cover and refrigerate overnight. The next day, divide dough into 10 to 12 balls. On a floured pastry sheet, roll out each ball into a 14-inch by 3-inch rectangle with a rolling pin. Take a tablespoonful of filling; roll in a little flour and place along the center of dough strip. Fold dough over filling. Moisten one edge of dough with a little water; bring edges together and press to seal. Repeat with remaining dough and filling. Place rolls seam-side down on a parchment paper-lined baking sheets, 2 inches apart. Brush with beaten egg; sprinkle with sugar. Bake at 425 degrees for 20 to 25 minutes, until golden. Slice and serve. Serves 6 to 8.

Delight your family with a few of Grandma's best recipes...
tuck recipe cards into a vintage pastry blender.

# Grandma's Best Christmas RECIPES

## Christmas Cheesy Swiss Pie

*Sheri Kohl*
*Wentzville, MO*

*My family looks forward to this every Christmas morning! I make one pie with ham and one with bacon. Any leftovers are cut into wedges, wrapped and frozen...they heat up nicely in the microwave.*

2 9-inch refrigerated deep-dish
   pie crusts, unbaked
1/4 c. cooked ham, bacon or
   sausage, chopped and divided
1-1/2 lbs. Swiss cheese,
   shredded and divided

6 eggs, beaten
3 c. half-and-half
1/4 t. nutmeg
1/4 t. salt
1/4 t. pepper

Place pie crusts on a baking sheet. Bake at 425 degrees for 7 to 8 minutes, until lightly golden. Remove from oven. Divide chopped meat between crusts, covering bottoms of crusts. Divide cheese between crusts; pack in cheese to fill crusts and set aside. In a large bowl, beat together eggs, half-and-half and seasonings. Pour into crusts, dividing evenly. Bake, uncovered, at 425 degrees for 15 minutes, then at 325 degrees for 30 to 45 minutes, until set in the center. Let stand several minutes, then cut into wedges. Makes 2 pies; each serves 6 to 8.

Serve up freshly baked muffins anytime. Place muffins in a freezer bag and freeze. To warm frozen muffins, wrap in heavy aluminum foil and pop into a 300-degree oven for 12 to 15 minutes.

# Waking Up at Grandma's

## Gram's Christmas Biscuit Ring

Sandy Coffey
Cincinnati, OH

*When the grandkids come to spend the night, they look forward to this special breakfast ring. A side of fruit and hot chocolate with a candy cane for stirring makes a fun Christmas breakfast.*

1/2 c. butter, melted
2 T. cinnamon
1/2 c. sugar

2 8-oz. tubes refrigerated
buttermilk biscuits

Add melted butter to a shallow dish; combine cinnamon and sugar in another shallow dish. Dip each biscuit into butter, then into cinnamon-sugar. Coat a Bundt® pan with non-stick vegetable spray. Arrange biscuits in pan, with biscuits standing up on end. Drizzle biscuits with any remaining butter and cinnamon-sugar. Bake at 350 degrees for 25 minutes. Turn upside-down onto a cake plate; serve warm. Makes 8 servings.

## Night Before Christmas Sticky Buns

Crystal Branstrom
Russell, PA

*A family favorite for Christmas brunch. It's my favorite too, as the recipe is prepared the night before Christmas!*

1 c. chopped walnuts
24 frozen dinner rolls
1 c. brown sugar, packed
1/2 c. butter

1/2 c. milk
3-oz. pkg. cook & serve vanilla
pudding mix
cinnamon to taste

Spread walnuts in a lightly greased 13"x9" baking pan. Arrange frozen rolls evenly over nuts; set aside. In a saucepan, combine brown sugar, butter, milk and pudding mix; bring to a boil. Pour mixture evenly over rolls. Cover and refrigerate overnight. The next morning, remove rolls from refrigerator. Uncover; sprinkle with cinnamon and let rise for 15 minutes. Bake at 350 degrees for 15 minutes, or until golden. Turn out onto a plate and serve. Makes 2 dozen.

## Christmas Eggnog Coffee Cake

*Judy Phelan*
*Macomb, IL*

*My husband Ed belongs to a morning men's group at church. They like to have something to go along with the coffee, first thing, and this is coffee cake is ideal to serve in December. Allow yourself enough time, as it needs to be refrigerated before baking.*

1/2 c. butter, softened
1 c. sugar
1 c. dairy eggnog
8-oz. container sour cream
2 eggs, beaten
1 t. rum extract

2-1/2 c. all-purpose flour
1-1/2 t. baking powder
1/2 t. baking soda
1/2 t. salt
1 to 2 t. shortening

Prepare Topping; set aside. In a large bowl, beat butter and sugar with an electric mixer on medium speed until blended. Beat in eggnog, sour cream, eggs and extract until well blended. Stir in remaining ingredients except shortening. Coat the bottom of a 13"x9" baking pan with shortening; pour batter into pan. Sprinkle topping over batter. Cover and refrigerate at least 8 hours. Uncover; bake at 350 degrees for 35 to 40 minutes, until a toothpick comes out clean. Cool for 20 minutes; drizzle with Glaze and cut into squares. Serves 15.

## Topping:

1/3 c. sugar
1 T. all-purpose flour

1 T. butter
1/2 t. nutmeg

Mix all ingredients with a fork until crumbly.

## Glaze:

1/2 c. powdered sugar

1 to 2 T. dairy eggnog

Mix together powdered sugar and eggnog until smooth and thin enough to drizzle.

# Waking Up at Grandma's

## Best Baked Oatmeal

*Karen Rowe*
*Carlisle, PA*

*When I married my husband 33 years ago, we settled in his hometown in south central Pennsylvania. There were many foods in this new town that I had never heard of, and baked oatmeal was one of them. A friend served it and I was hooked! Over the years, I changed some of the ingredients, now it's an expected dish for family gatherings and Christmas morning.*

1 c. butter
4 eggs, beaten
2 c. milk
2 t. vanilla extract
2 c. brown sugar, packed
1-1/2 T. baking powder
1-1/2 t. cinnamon
6 c. old-fashioned oats, uncooked
Optional: chopped nuts, raisins or cranberries, semi-sweet or white chocolate chips

Melt butter in a large microwave-safe bowl. Add remaining ingredients except oats and optional ingredients; stir well. Fold in oats and optional ingredients, if using. Spoon mixture into a buttered 13"x9" baking pan. Bake, uncovered, at 350 degrees for 40 to 45 minutes, until firm in the center. Makes 12 servings.

Make the countdown to Christmas a treat! Hide trinkets in goodie bags, or hang wrapped gingerbread men on an Advent calendar. Terrific ways to give the kids something to look forward to each day.

## Southern Breakfast Casserole

*Leslie Nagel*
*Noxapater, MS*

*This is one of our family's favorite breakfast casseroles. It's great on Christmas morning! For a spicy variation, add a drained can of diced tomatoes with green chiles.*

1 lb. ground pork sausage
3 c. water
3/4 c. quick-cooking grits, uncooked
5-oz. can evaporated milk

1/4 t. garlic powder
1/4 t. pepper
8-oz. pkg. shredded Cheddar cheese, divided
2 eggs, well beaten

Brown sausage in a skillet over medium heat; drain well. Meanwhile, bring water to a boil in a large saucepan over medium-high heat; slowly stir in grits. Reduce heat to medium-low; cover and cook for 6 minutes, stirring occasionally. Remove from heat. Add evaporated milk, garlic powder, pepper and 1-1/2 cups cheese. Stir well until cheese is melted; stir in browned sausage and eggs. Transfer to a lightly greased 13"x9" baking pan. Bake, uncovered, at 350 degrees for 50 minutes. Sprinkle remaining cheese on top; bake for another 5 minutes. Let stand for 8 to 10 minutes before serving. Makes 12 to 15 servings.

Hosting a Christmas brunch? Add a festive note with your favorite Bundt®cake...it can double as a dessert and decoration.

## Almond Tea

*Debbie Driggers*
*Campbell, TX*

*My mother and my grandmother used to make this every Christmas. Mom has been gone for 27 years now, so this recipe is very special, and my sister and I make it for our families at Christmas. It is good hot or chilled, and can be made ahead and frozen until ready to use.*

12-1/2 c. water, divided
4 family-size tea bags
2 c. sugar
1/4 c. lemon juice
46-oz. can sweetened
    pineapple juice

1/2 c. powdered orange
    drink mix
1-1/2 t. almond extract
1-1/2 t. vanilla extract

Add 3-1/2 cups water to a large saucepan over high heat. Bring to a boil; remove from heat. Add tea bags; let stand for 5 minutes. Discard tea bags. Meanwhile, in another large saucepan, combine 6 cups water, sugar and lemon juice. Simmer over medium heat for 5 minutes, stirring until sugar dissolves; let cool. Add brewed tea, pineapple juice, orange drink mix, extracts and remaining 3 cups water. Stir until combined. Serve hot or chilled; freezes well. Makes 12 to 15 servings.

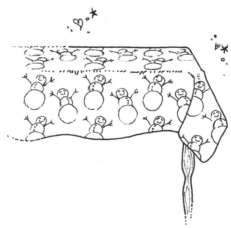

A vintage-style oilcloth tablecloth with brightly colored reindeer or snowmen is oh-so cheerful at breakfast... sticky syrup and jam spills are easily wiped off with a damp sponge!

## Slow-Cooker Blueberry Breakfast Casserole

*Amy Moats*
*Hart, MI*

*This is a family favorite on chilly mornings. It stores well in the refrigerator and makes a busy morning easy...just warm it up and serve. The casserole is crumbly when warm and sliceable when cool.*

2 c. fresh or frozen blueberries
1 egg, beaten
1 c. hot wheat cereal, uncooked
1 c. long-cooking oats, uncooked
1 t. baking powder
1 c. brown sugar, packed
1 c. all-purpose flour
1/2 t. salt
1/4 c. oil
1/4 c. chopped walnuts
3 T. butter, melted
1 c. milk
cinnamon to taste
Optional: mixed berries, cranberries, sliced strawberries, chopped pecans or almonds, orange zest
Garnish: milk or cream

In a 4-quart slow cooker, combine all except optional ingredients and garnish; stir well. Fold in optional ingredients as desired. Cover and cook on low setting for 3 hours, or on high setting for 1-1/2 hours. Serve warm, topped with milk or cream. Makes 10 servings.

For extra-special pancakes and waffles, whip up some maple butter in no time. Just blend 1/2 cup softened butter with 3/4 cup maple syrup.

# Waking Up at Grandma's

## Easy Danish Kringle

*Joan Baker*
*Westland, MI*

*A friend gave me this recipe. It is oh-so good at brunch...one of the first things to go! Makes a great breakfast bread too. Use your favorite nuts...pecans, almonds and walnuts are all good.*

9-inch refrigerated pie crust
2/3 c. chopped nuts
1/2 c. brown sugar, packed
3 T. butter, softened
1/2 c. powdered sugar
1/4 t. vanilla extract
2 to 3 t. milk
Optional: 3 T. additional
    chopped nuts

Unroll crust onto an ungreased large baking sheet; set aside. In a bowl, combine nuts, brown sugar and butter. Sprinkle mixture over 1/2 of crust to within 3/4 inch of edge. Brush edge of crust with water; fold pie crust over filling. Move pastry to center of baking sheet. Seal edge with a fork. Pierce top several times with fork. Bake at 375 degrees for 17 to 22 minutes, until golden. Allow to cool for 5 minutes. In a small bowl, mix powdered sugar, vanilla and enough milk to make a smooth, drizzling consistency. Drizzle icing over warm pastry; if desired, sprinkle with additional nuts. Cool completely for about 30 minutes, cut into wedges. Serves 6.

Fasten cookie cutters to a pine garland with ribbon bows...
so charming in the kitchen!

# Grandma's Best
# Christmas
## RECIPES

## Grandma's Hashbrowns

*Jeannie Stone*
*Nova Scotia, Canada*

*My mom made this for breakfast based on her mother's hashbrowns.
Now I make it, based it on my mom's. So it changed in three
generations...who knows how my daughter will change it again!*

30-oz. pkg. frozen shredded
   hashbrowns
10-3/4 oz. can cream of celery
   soup
8-oz. container sour cream onion
   chip dip

1 c. shredded Cheddar cheese
1 c. cooked bacon, ham or
   sausage, chopped

Combine all ingredients in a large bowl and mix well. Transfer to a
lightly greased 3-quart casserole dish. Cover and refrigerate overnight.
Bake, covered, at 375 degrees for 45 minutes, or until hot and bubbly.
Makes 8 servings.

Grandma's favorite salt & pepper shakers, in the shape of
Santa & Mrs. Santa, add a touch of holiday cheer to any
buffet table and a smile to guests' faces.

# Waking Up
# at Grandma's

## Baked French Eggs

*Joan Raven*
*Cicero, NY*

*Our family has been enjoying baked French eggs for years! It just wouldn't be Christmas breakfast without this egg bake coming out of the oven for everyone to enjoy, especially after opening our Christmas presents! This is a snap to prepare, and takes just minutes to bake. Serve alongside crisp bacon and hearty toast with homemade Christmas jam...delish!*

1 doz. eggs
1/2 c. whipping cream
salt and pepper to taste

8-oz. pkg. shredded Parmigiano
cheese

Generously spray 12 muffin cups with non-stick butter-flavored spray. Crack one egg into each cup. Drizzle each egg with 2 teaspoons cream; season with salt and pepper and sprinkle with one tablespoon cheese. Bake, uncovered, at 425 degrees, 7 to 8 minutes for soft consistency, 9 to 10 minutes for semi-soft or 11 to 12 minutes for firm. Serve immediately. Makes 6 servings.

## Supreme Scrambled Eggs

*Janis Parr*
*Ontario, Canada*

*This recipe takes scrambled eggs to the next level!*
*They're creamy and delicious when prepared this way.*

8 eggs
1-1/2 T. mayonnaise
4 t. all-purpose flour

1/8 t. salt
1 T. butter
2 t. fresh chives, finely chopped

In a bowl, whisk together eggs, mayonnaise, flour and salt until smooth. Melt butter in large skillet over medium heat until skillet is hot. Add eggs. Cook, stirring occasionally, until eggs are cooked through. Top with fresh chives and serve. Makes 4 servings.

## Ginny's Bacon Quiche

*Margaret McNeil*
*Germantown, TN*

*My cousin Ginny shared this recipe with me in the fall of 2000. Later that year, I made it for Christmas morning. Little did I know that I'd created a family tradition! This will be the 23rd year that this quiche has been our breakfast on Christmas Day.*

2  9-inch refrigerated pie crusts
2 to 3 t. all-purpose flour
6 eggs, beaten
2 c. milk
salt and pepper to taste

12-oz. pkg. sliced bacon, crisply cooked and crumbled
8-oz. pkg. shredded Cheddar cheese

Fit both pie crusts side-by-side into an ungreased 13"x9" glass baking pan; pinch seams to seal. Trim crusts. Sprinkle flour over bottoms and sides of pie crusts; set aside. In a large bowl, whisk together eggs, milk and seasonings. Fold in bacon and cheese; spoon mixture into crusts in pan. (Filling ingredients may be assembled the night before and stored in the refrigerator.) Bake, uncovered, at 375 degrees for 40 to 45 minutes, until set. Cut into squares and serve. Serves 6 to 8.

Early in the holiday season, check your spice rack for freshness. Crush a pinch of each spice...if it has a fresh, zingy scent, it's still good. Toss out any old-smelling spices and stock up on ones you've used up during the year.

# Waking Up at Grandma's

## Tracey's Crustless Quiche

*Lisa Ashton*
*Aston, PA*

*My friend Tracey gave me this recipe a long time ago. My daughter,*
*who does not like pie crust, loves this recipe!*

5 eggs
1-1/2 c. milk
1/4 c. butter, melted
salt and pepper to taste

1/2 c. pancake mix
1/2 c. shredded Cheddar cheese
1/2 c. cooked bacon, ham or
  sausage, chopped

In a large bowl, beat eggs by hand. Add milk, slowly whisking to combine. Stir in melted butter, salt and pepper. Add pancake mix, cheese and and meat; mix well. Pour into a greased 9" pie plate. Bake, uncovered, at 350 degrees for 45 minutes, or until set. Let stand for about 15 minutes; cut into wedges. Makes 6 servings.

## Christmas Morning Punch

*Ann Farris*
*Biscoe, AR*

*This is called Christmas punch, but we have it for Christmas Eve,*
*Christmas Eve Eve...any time we can! Once you try this,*
*you will be addicted.*

2 c. orange juice
2 c. cranberry juice
1 c. pineapple juice

1 c. ginger ale
Optional: grated fresh ginger
  to taste

Mix all ingredients in a pitcher; cover and chill. Serve cold. Makes 8 servings.

A merry Christmas to everybody!
A happy New Year to all the world!
– Charles Dickens

## Amazing Orange Apricot Bread

*Janis Parr*
*Ontario, Canada*

*Apricot bread is a favorite of mine. This recipe yields
a moist and delicious loaf that freezes well, too.*

1 c. dried apricots, finely chopped
3 T. butter, softened
1 c. sugar
2 T. brown sugar, packed
1 egg, beaten
1 t. vanilla extract
3/4 c. orange juice

2 c. all-purpose flour
2 t. baking powder
1/2 t. baking soda
3/4 t. salt
1/2 t. cinnamon
1/4 t. ground ginger

In a bowl, cover apricots with hot water; let stand for 15 minutes to soften. Drain well; pat apricots dry with paper towels. In a large bowl, blend together butter and sugars well. Stir in egg, vanilla, orange juice and apricots. In another bowl, whisk together flour, baking powder, baking soda, salt and spices. Add flour mixture to orange juice mixture, stirring only until combined. Pour batter into a greased 9"x5" loaf pan. Bake at 350 degrees for 55 to 60 minutes, until a toothpick inserted in the center tests done. Set pan on a wire rack to cool; turn out loaf and slice. Makes one loaf.

Take time to invite a friend over for afternoon tea. Serve freshly baked muffins or fruit bread with a steaming pot of tea... a great way to catch up during the holidays!

# Waking Up at Grandma's

## Lisa's Berry-Berry Muffins

*Lisa Ann Panzino DiNunzio*
*Vineland, NJ*

*A perfect muffin to serve Christmas morning, or any day of the year...they're so delicious!*

1-3/4 c. all-purpose flour
3/4 c. sugar
2 T. baking powder
1/2 t. salt
3/4 c. milk
1/3 c. oil

1 egg, beaten
1 t. vanilla extract
1/2 c. fresh or frozen blueberries
1/2 c. fresh or frozen cranberries
Optional: additional sugar

In a large bowl, stir together flour, sugar, baking powder and salt; set aside. In a separate bowl, whisk together milk, oil, egg, and vanilla. Add milk mixture to flour mixture; stir just until combined. Gently stir in blueberries and cranberries. Fill greased or paper-lined muffin cups 3/4 full with batter. Sprinkle each muffin with a little additional sugar, if desired. Bake at 400 degrees for 20 minutes, or until a toothpick inserted into the center of muffins comes out clean. Makes one dozen.

If the baking powder in the cupboard is from last Christmas, it may be best to replace it...baking soda, too. Test it by stirring a teaspoonful into a mug of very hot water. If it fizzes, it's still good to use.

## Mimie's Slow-Cooker Hot Chocolate

*Beckie Apple*
*Grannis, AR*

*My Mimie was a schoolteacher for more than half her life. She loved children, and of course her grandchildren (including me!) were at the top of her list. We loved her famous hot chocolate. I have now converted it to a slow-cooker recipe. Great for a holiday morning... add some candy canes for stirring!*

8 c. whole or 2% milk
12-oz. pkg. milk chocolate chips
5 T. vanilla extract
14-oz. can sweetened
    condensed milk

12-oz. can evaporated milk
1/2 t. cinnamon
4 c. mini marshmallows

In a 4-quart slow cooker, combine all ingredients except marshmallows; stir well. Cover and cook on high setting for 1-1/2 hours, stirring often, until chocolate chips have melted and all ingredients are well combined. Top with marshmallows; cover and cook for another 30 to 45 minutes. Ladle into mugs; serve hot. Makes 8 to 10 servings.

Buttery cinnamon toast warms you right up on a chilly morning... perfect with a mug of hot cocoa! Spread softened butter generously on one side of toasted bread and sprinkle with cinnamon-sugar. Broil for one to 2 minutes, until hot and bubbly. Just like Grandma used to make!

# Waking Up at Grandma's

## Pecan-Pumpkin Spice Muffins

*Laura Fuller*
*Fort Wayne, IN*

*Grammy's favorite muffins...she always made them for the holidays.*

| | |
|---|---|
| 1/2 c. raisins | 1/4 t. nutmeg |
| 1 c. boiling water | 2 eggs, beaten |
| 1-1/2 c. self-rising flour | 3/4 c. oil |
| 1 c. sugar | 1/2 c. canned pumpkin |
| 1/2 t. cinnamon | 1/2 c. chopped pecans |

In a small bowl, cover raisins with boiling water. Set aside for 5 minutes. Meanwhile, in a large bowl, mix flour, sugar and spices. Add eggs, oil and pumpkin; stir just until combined. Drain raisins; fold into batter along with pecans. Pour batter into 12 greased muffin cups, filling 2/3 full. Bake at 350 degrees for 25 minutes, or until a toothpick inserted in center tests clean. Serve warm or at room temperature. Makes one dozen.

## Holiday Coffee Cake

*Lenore Pfaff*
*Miles City, MT*

*Serve topped with butter...what a wonderful way to start the day!*

| | |
|---|---|
| 18-1/2 oz. pkg. yellow cake mix | 3-3/4 c. powdered sugar |
| 3 eggs, divided | 1 t. vanilla extract |
| 1/2 c. butter, softened | 1/4 to 1/2 c. sliced almonds |
| 8-oz. pkg. cream cheese, softened | |

In a large bowl, combine dry cake mix, one beaten egg and butter; mix well. Pat into the bottom of a greased 13"x9" baking pan; set aside. In a separate bowl, mix remaining beaten eggs, cream cheese, powdered sugar and vanilla; spoon over cake mixture in pan. Sprinkle almonds on top. Bake at 350 degrees for 25 minutes; cut into squares. Serve warm. Makes 15 servings.

## Biscuits & Gravy Roll-Ups

*Tina Goodpasture*
*Meadowview, VA*

*My Granny Hudson made the best gravy around. The bread she made we called "morning bread." She rolled it out and baked it, we just tore off a piece. It was the best ever! Granny kept food on the table all day long, covered with a tablecloth. Whenever someone came to see her, she already had food ready. You were to eat whether you were hungry or not! She loved to feed folks and to watch them eat. More than 60 years later, I still remember the wonderful tastes and smells of Granny's kitchen.*

1 lb. mild ground pork
   breakfast sausage
8-oz. pkg. cream cheese,
   softened

8-oz. tube refrigerated crescent
   dough sheet

Brown sausage in a skillet over medium heat; drain and stir in cream cheese. Unroll crescent dough; spread sausage mixture over dough all the way to the edge. Roll up dough lengthwise; refrigerate until firm. If baking the next day, wrap roll in parchment paper and aluminum foil; refrigerate overnight. Slice chilled roll into 1/4-inch rounds; arrange on a lightly greased baking sheet. Bake, uncovered, at 375 degrees for 15 minutes, or until golden. Serves 6.

A sweet keepsake for a family brunch. Copy one of Grandma's tried & true recipes onto a festive card, then punch a hole in the corner and tie the card to a rolled napkin with a length of ribbon.

## Debbie's Strawberry Bread

*Debbie Adkins*
*Nicholasville, KY*

*While most people make pumpkin bread during the holidays,
I make this instead. I've been making it for almost 40 years...
it's perfect for gift baskets!*

1-1/2 c. all-purpose flour
1-1/2 c. sugar
1/2 t. baking soda
1/2 t. salt
1-1/2 t. cinnamon

2 eggs, lightly beaten
1/2 c. plus 2 T. canola oil
10-oz. pkg. frozen sweetened
    sliced strawberries, thawed

In a large bowl, combine flour, sugar, baking soda, salt and cinnamon.
Mix well and set aside. In another large bowl, combine eggs and oil.
Beat with an electric mixer on low speed until combined. Add flour
mixture to egg mixture; beat on low speed just until combined. With
a spoon, stir in strawberries. Pour batter into a greased and floured
9"x5" loaf pan. Bake at 350 degrees for 50 to 60 minutes, until a
toothpick inserted in center comes out clean. Cool in pan on a wire
rack; turn out of pan. Makes one loaf.

A gift of homemade fruit bread is always welcome...it can even
be made ahead one to 2 months and frozen. To keep it oven-fresh,
let the bread cool completely before wrapping first in aluminum
foil, then in plastic wrap.

# Grandma's Best *Christmas* RECIPES

## Overnight Fruit Pastry

*Roxanne Anderson*
*Williams, IA*

*This recipe came from my aunt, and I have been making it for years. My daughter made it for years, too. It is easy to mix it up the night before, then roll out and bake on Christmas morning before everyone else wakes up.*

1 c. warm milk, about 110 to
  115 degrees
1 cake fresh yeast, or 1 env.
  active dry yeast
4 egg yolks, beaten
1 t. salt

3-1/2 c. all-purpose flour
1/3 c. sugar
1 c. butter, softened
2 12-oz. cans favorite fruit
  pastry filling, divided

In a bowl, combine warm milk, yeast, egg yolks and salt; set aside. In a separate bowl, combine flour, sugar and softened butter; mix with a pastry blender until mixture resembles small crumbs. Pour milk mixture into flour mixture; stir just until blended. Cover bowl with plastic wrap; refrigerate overnight. When ready to bake, divide dough into 4 equal parts. On a floured surface, roll out each part into an 18-inch by 12-inch rectangle. Spread 1/2 can pastry filling over rectangle. Roll rectangle into a log, starting with one long edge. Repeat with remaining dough and filling. Place rolled logs onto baking sheets sprayed with non-stick vegetable spray. With a sharp knife, cut a slit lengthwise down the center of each log without cutting all the way through. Bake at 350 degrees for 20 minutes. While still warm, drizzle with Powdered Sugar Icing. Cut into one-inch slices. Makes about 3-1/2 dozen.

## Powdered Sugar Icing:

1-1/2 c. powdered sugar
1/2 t. vanilla extract

1 T. milk, or more as needed

Stir together all ingredients, adding milk to desired consistency.

God bless us, every one!
–Charles Dickens

# Waking Up at Grandma's

## Overnight Sausage Brunch Casserole

*Hollie Moots*
*Marysville, OH*

*My grandma made this for many family breakfast gatherings, and shared the recipe with me. It has become a staple for the holidays now, being made by three more generations!*

1 lb. ground pork sausage
6 eggs
2 c. milk
1 c. shredded sharp Cheddar
   cheese

1 t. dry mustard
6 slices bread, cubed

The night before, brown sausage in a skillet over medium heat; drain. Transfer sausage to a covered container; refrigerate overnight. In a large bowl, beat eggs; whisk in milk, cheese and mustard. Add bread cubes and stir to combine. Cover and refrigerate overnight. In the morning, spread sausage evenly in a greased 13"x9" baking pan. Pour egg mixture over sausage. Bake, uncovered, at 350 degrees for 45 to 60 minutes, until set and top is golden. Serves 10 to 12.

Legend has it that burning a bayberry candle on Christmas Eve brings good luck throughout the new year. Stack ribbon-tied bundles of candles in a basket...a pretty decoration that doubles as gifts for visitors.

## Marion's Caramel Rolls

Karen Antonides
Gahanna, OH

*This is a recipe that I got from my mother-in-law Marion, many years ago. It is a favorite of all five of her children, and a recipe that my husband couldn't stop talking about. It tastes homemade, but it uses frozen bread dough and is much easier to make. During a visit, I had Marion show me exactly how it was made, so I could make it for my husband and family. Whenever his brothers and sisters come to visit, I try to have a pan of caramel rolls ready to enjoy and reminisce about what a special and humorous lady she was.*

1 c. sugar
2 t. cinnamon
1/3 to 1/2 c. brown sugar,
    packed
1/2 c. chopped walnuts

1 t. corn syrup
1/2 t. water
2 loaves frozen bread dough,
    thawed
1/2 c. margarine, melted

Mix together sugar and cinnamon in a shallow bowl; set aside. Sprinkle brown sugar into a 13"x9" baking pan sprayed with non-stick vegetable spray; add walnuts. Drizzle corn syrup over walnuts; sprinkle with water and set aside. Cut each thawed loaf into 6 pieces. Stretch each piece of dough into an 8-inch rope. Drench each rope in melted margarine; roll in cinnamon-sugar and tie rope in a knot. Arrange rolls in pan over walnut mixture. Cover with a towel; let rise in a warm place until double. Bake at 350 degrees for 30 minutes, or until golden. Brush remaining margarine over hot rolls; let cool for 10 minutes. Turn pan over to release rolls onto a platter; allow caramel sauce to run over rolls. Makes one dozen.

Decorate the kitchen for the holidays! Tie cheery bows on cabinet knobs, hang cookie cutters in the window and tuck sprigs of fresh pine into sifters or canisters.

# Waking Up
# at Grandma's

## Spiced Christmas Coffee

*Kathy Grashoff*
*Fort Wayne, IN*

*Perfect for a special breakfast or brunch.*

10 c. hot brewed coffee
1/3 c. water
1/2 c. sugar
1/4 c. baking cocoa
1/4 t. cinnamon
1/8 t. nutmeg
Garnish: sweetened whipped
   cream

Keep brewed coffee warm in a large saucepan. In a small saucepan over medium heat, bring water to a low boil. Stir in sugar, cocoa and spices. Return to a low boil for about one minute until syrupy, stirring occasionally. Add to hot coffee in saucepan; mix well. Pour coffee into mugs and top with whipped cream. Makes 10 servings.

## Kmee Cakes

*Kathleen Murray Strunk*
*Chandler, AZ*

*This pancake recipe is our favorite. My sweet granddaughter Bethany and I make them when she spends the weekend. Kmee is my grandma's name, so my granddaughter calls them Kmee Cakes. She likes hers served with sweetened whipped cream and lots of candy sprinkles! We think the best times together are those spent in the kitchen.*

1 egg
1 c. all-purpose flour
1-1/4 c. plain Greek yogurt
5 T. milk
2 T. extra-virgin olive oil
1 T. brown sugar, packed
2 t. baking powder
1/4 t. baking soda
1/2 t. kosher salt
2 T. butter

In a large bowl, whisk egg until fluffy. Beat in remaining ingredients except butter until almost smooth. Be careful not to overbeat; batter will be thick. Melt butter in an electric skillet set at 325 degrees. Add 1/3 cup batter per pancake to pan; smooth batter with a spatula as needed. Cook pancakes until edges begin to bubble and look dry. Turn and cook the other side until golden. Makes about one dozen pancakes.

# Grandma's Best *Christmas* RECIPES

## Mississippi Breakfast Casserole

*Stephanie McClintock*
*Falkner, MS*

*When I was growing up, Mom would always bake this casserole on Christmas morning. It's a great make-ahead recipe, since it's put together the night before the morning you need to bake it.*

6 slices white or wheat bread,
    crusts trimmed
1 T. butter, softened
1 lb. ground pork sausage
8-oz. pkg. shredded
    Cheddar cheese

6 eggs, beaten
2 c. half-and-half
1/2 t. salt
1/2 t. pepper

Spread one side of each bread slice with butter. Arrange slices, butter-side up, in a greased 13"x9" baking pan; set aside. Brown sausage in a skillet over medium heat; drain. Spoon sausage over bread; sprinkle cheese over sausage. Whisk together remaining ingredients in a bowl; spoon over cheese. Cover and refrigerate for 8 hours. In the morning, uncover; let stand at room temperature for 30 minutes. Bake, uncovered, at 350 degrees for 45 minutes, or until heated through and golden on top. Makes 8 servings.

A countertop mug rack makes a fun display rack for cherished Christmas ornaments.

## Polly's Lemon Bread

*Lisa Cunningham*
*Boothbay, ME*

*This sweet and tangy recipe was my Aunt Polly's. Every year she would make it around the holidays, but it really is good year 'round. Delicious with breakfast on Christmas morning...great for a family get-together before the holidays, too.*

| | |
|---|---|
| 1/4 c. shortening | 1 T. baking powder |
| 1 c. sugar | 1/2 t. salt |
| 2 eggs, beaten | zest of 1 lemon |
| 1-1/2 c. all-purpose flour | 1/c c. milk |

In a large bowl, blend shortening and sugar; add eggs and mix well. Add flour, baking powder, salt and zest; stir together. Add milk and mix again. Pour batter into a greased and floured 8"x8" baking pan. Bake at 350 degrees for 55 minutes. About 10 minutes before done, remove from oven; pierce cake several times with a fork. Spoon Lemon Glaze over the top; return to oven for 10 minutes. Makes 8 servings.

### Lemon Glaze:

| | |
|---|---|
| juice of 1 lemon | 1/2 c. sugar |

Combine juice and sugar in a saucepan. Cook and stir over low heat until sugar is fully dissolved.

The smallest holes in a cheese grater work well for lemon or orange zest in a jiffy. No grater? Simply use a vegetable peeler to remove very thin slices of peel, then mince finely with a paring knife.

# Grandma's Best *Christmas* RECIPES

## Freda's Coffee Cake

*Wendy Paffenroth*
*Pine Island, NY*

*When I was growing up, we had a neighbor up the street whose grandchildren didn't live nearby, so my sisters and I became her adopted grandchildren. Mrs. Schoonmaker was a great baker, and often I was at her house watching and learning. She even had a special apron for me. This delicious recipe of hers is from the 1960s, and to this day, it's a family favorite.*

1/2 c. butter, softened
1 c. sugar
2 eggs, beaten
1 c. sour cream
1 t. baking soda

1-1/2 c. all-purpose flour
1-1/2 t. baking powder
1 t. vanilla extract
Optional: powdered sugar

In a large bowl, beat together butter and sugar. Add eggs; beat until light and smooth. In another bowl, combine sour cream and baking soda; add to butter mixture and beat again. Beat in flour, baking powder and vanilla. Pour half of batter into a greased tube pan; sprinkle with Topping and add remaining batter. Bake at 350 degrees for 45 minutes, or until top springs back when touched. Turn off oven; open door slightly and allow cake to cool in oven for one hour. Turn out onto a serving plate. If desired, dust with powdered sugar; slice to serve. Makes 8 servings.

## Topping:

1/2 c. sugar
1 t. baking cocoa

1 t. cinnamon
1/3 c. chopped pecans or walnuts

Mix all ingredients well.

# Waking Up at Grandma's

## Grandmother's Fruit Salad

*Tracee Cummins*
*Georgetown, TX*

*My great-grandmother was the best cook and sweetest woman in the world! She always made every meal an occasion. This was one of her favorite salad recipes. It has become known in our family as Grandmother's Christmas Salad because we always make it at Christmas in her memory. The creamy dressing makes this recipe a standout.*

8-oz. can pineapple tidbits,
    drained and 1/3 cup juice
    reserved
15-oz. can fruit cocktail, drained
2 bananas, diced
1 c. mini marshmallows

1/2 c. butter
1/2 c. sugar
1 T. all-purpose flour
1 egg, beaten
1 c. whipping cream

Combine pineapple, fruit cocktail, bananas and marshmallows in a bowl; set aside. In a saucepan over medium heat, mix butter, sugar, flour, egg and reserved pineapple juice; bring to a boil. Cook and stir until thickened. Remove from heat; set aside to cool. In a deep bowl, beat cream with an electric mixer on medium speed until soft peaks form. Fold whipped cream into warm butter mixture; add to fruit mixture and mix gently. Cover and chill before serving. Makes 8 servings.

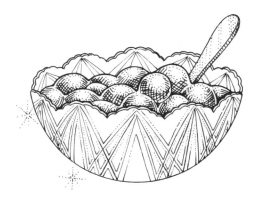

The bright colors of fresh fruit really shine in Grandma's prettiest vintage cut-glass bowl. When washing cut glass, add a little white vinegar to the rinse water...the glass will sparkle!

## Best Overnight French Toast

*Barb Butler*
*Schoolcraft, MI*

*At our house, Christmas morning breakfast is always special.*
*I've been making this for the past four years. People rave about it*
*and always go back for more!*

1 loaf French bread, sliced
   1-inch thick
8 eggs, beaten
1 c. half-and-half
1/2 c. milk

2 T. sugar
1 T. vanilla extract
1/2 t. cinnamon
1/4 t. nutmeg
1/4 t. salt

Arrange bread slices in a greased 13"x9" baking pan, making 2 rows and overlapping slices; set aside. In a large bowl, whisk together remaining ingredients until combined. Spoon over bread, making sure to cover all. Cover with aluminum foil; refrigerate overnight. Just before baking, uncover; spread Praline Topping evenly over bread. Bake at 350 degrees for 40 minutes, or until puffy and lightly golden. Makes 8 servings.

## Praline Topping:

1 c. butter, room temperature
1 c. brown sugar, packed
1 c. chopped pecans

1/2 t. cinnamon
1/2 t. nutmeg

Combine all ingredients; mix thoroughly.

Aprons are practical, but also adorable! Look for the 1950s style with poinsettias, snowmen and Santa Claus...perfect gifts for girlfriends who love to cook.

# Waking Up
## at Grandma's

## Sausage & Rice Casserole

*Elizabeth Smithson*
*Mayfield, KY*

*My daughter has always brought this dish for our Christmas brunch.*
*It's always a treat...everyone loves it!*

1 lb. ground pork hot sausage,
   browned and drained
10-3/4 oz. can cream of
   mushroom soup
10-3/4 oz. can cream of chicken
   soup

3/4 c. milk
3 c. cooked rice
16-oz. pkg. pasteurized process
   cheese, cubed, or 16-oz. jar
   pasteurized process cheese
   sauce

Combine all ingredients in a large bowl; mix well. Spread evenly in a
lightly greased 13"x9" baking pan. Bake, uncovered, at 350 degrees for
30 to 40 minutes, until hot and bubbly. Makes 24 servings.

Celebrate the season with a holiday brunch buffet for friends
and neighbors! For a midday brunch, offer a light, savory main
dish or 2 alongside breakfast foods like baked eggs, coffee cake
and muffins. Guests who have already enjoyed breakfast
will appreciate it.

# Grandma's Best *Christmas* RECIPES

## Eggnog Holiday Bread

*Shirley Howie*
*Foxboro, MA*

*This is a very festive, light loaf that's perfect for those who aren't fond of the heavier, traditional fruitcake. I make it to serve alongside our leisurely Christmas brunch, which we enjoy just before opening our presents!*

3 c. all-purpose flour
3/4 c. sugar
1 T. baking powder
1/2 t. salt
1/2 t. nutmeg
1-1/2 c. dairy eggnog,
   slightly warmed

1 egg, beaten
1 t. vanilla extract
1/4 c. butter, melted
3/4 c. chopped pecans
3/4 c. candied fruit

In a large bowl, mix together flour, sugar, baking powder, salt and nutmeg until well combined. In a separate bowl, mix together eggnog, egg, vanilla and butter. Add eggnog mixture to flour mixture, stirring well. Stir in pecans and candied fruit. Pour batter into a greased 9"x5" loaf pan. Bake at 350 degrees for about 60 minutes, until a cake tester inserted in center comes out clean. Cool in pan on a wire rack; turn loaf out of pan. Makes one loaf.

In December, the principal household duty lies in preparing for the creature comforts of those near and dear to us.
—Isabella Beeton

# Family-Pleasing Sides & Salads

## Cousin Cora's Potatoes

*Laurie Malone*
*Crystal Lake, IL*

*This is an old recipe. My mom made these potatoes every December 24th when I was young. They went so well with the baked ham and the oven-fried chicken. I think I still have the brown casserole dish she used for this recipe! I have a feeling Yukon Gold potatoes would be delicious in this, too.*

8 russet potatoes, peeled
    and sliced
1/4 c. sliced pimentos, drained
1-1/2 c. shredded American
    cheese
3 T. yellow onion, finely chopped

2 t. salt
1/8 t. pepper
10-3/4 oz. can cream of
    mushroom soup
1 c. milk
2 T. butter, diced

Place sliced potatoes in a bowl of ice water. Let stand until potatoes are firm and crisp; drain well. In a lightly greased 2-quart casserole dish, layer half each of potatoes, pimentos, cheese, onion, salt and pepper. Repeat layering; set aside. Whisk together soup and milk in a bowl; spoon over potatoes. Dot with butter. Cover and bake at 325 degrees for one hour. Uncover; continue baking for one more hour. Makes 6 servings.

Early in December, go ahead and unpack Grandma's
Christmas tableware...even the simplest meal is special
when served on holly-trimmed plates.

# Family-Pleasing Sides & Salads

## Maple-Cranberry Sweet Potato Casserole

*Jo Ann Tobias*
*Cogan Station, PA*

*My mother-in-law brought some maple-glazed sweet potatoes to Christmas a few years ago. I loved the taste! I took the recipe and made it my own by introducing a few changes. If there happen to be leftovers, they heat up well.*

4 lbs. sweet potatoes, peeled
   and cubed
1 c. pure maple syrup
1-1/2 c. fresh cranberries

3 T. butter, plus more to taste
juice of 2 oranges
salt to taste
1 c. brown sugar

In a large saucepan, cover sweet potatoes with water. Cook over high heat until fork-tender; drain and cool slightly. Meanwhile, in another saucepan, heat maple syrup to boiling over high heat. Reduce heat to medium. Boil for 10 to 15 minutes, until syrup is reduced by half. Stir in cranberries, 3 tablespoons butter, orange juice and salt. Cook for about 5 minutes, until berries pop. Mash sweet potatoes with brown sugar and additional butter as desired. Spread in a lightly greased 13"x9" baking pan; spoon syrup mixture over top. Bake, uncovered, at 350 degrees for 20 minutes, or until heated through. Makes 10 servings.

Fresh cranberries can be kept frozen up to 12 months,
so if you enjoy them, stock up every autumn when
they're available and pop unopened bags in the freezer.
You'll be able to add their fruity tang to recipes year 'round.

# Grandma's Best *Christmas* RECIPES

## Genevieve's Green Bean Casserole

*Terri King*
*Georgetown, TX*

*My mother-in-law made this delicious side dish every year and now it's a regular at our holiday gatherings.*

9 T. butter, divided
6 T. all-purpose flour
3/4 c. onion, finely chopped
1-1/2 t. salt
cayenne pepper to taste
3 c. sour cream
2 7-oz. jars diced pimentos, drained

6 14-1/2 oz. cans cut green beans, well drained
1 c. shredded sharp Cheddar cheese
3 c. corn flake cereal, crushed

Melt 6 tablespoons butter in a skillet over low heat; blend in flour. Add onion, salt and cayenne pepper; stir until very smooth. Stir in sour cream and pimentos. Remove from heat; fold in green beans. Transfer mixture to a greased 1-1/2 quart casserole dish. Sprinkle with shredded cheese; sprinkle crushed corn flakes over cheese. Melt remaining butter; drizzle over top. Bake, uncovered, at 350 degrees for 30 minutes, or until hot and bubbly. Makes 12 servings.

Clip vintage Christmas cards onto pine garland with red clothespins for a festive mantel decoration.

# Family-Pleasing Sides & Salads

## Broccoli-Corn Casserole

*Stephanie Nilsen*
*Fremont, NE*

*This is Grandma's recipe that she served at family gatherings.
It is very tasty, and takes about five minutes to mix!*

14-3/4 oz. can creamed corn
10-oz. pkg. frozen chopped
  broccoli, thawed
1/2 t. salt

1/8 t. pepper
3/4 c. round buttery crackers,
  crushed an divided
4 T. butter, melted and divided

In a large bowl, mix all ingredients, setting aside 1/4 cup crushed crackers and 2 tablespoons melted butter for topping. Spread mixture in a greased 9"x9" baking pan. Mix reserved crumbs and butter; sprinkle over top. Cover and bake at 350 degrees for 30 minutes; uncover and bake another 15 minutes. Makes 8 servings.

## Easy-Peasy Veggie Casserole

*Judy Lange*
*Imperial, PA*

*An easy, tasty side for Sunday and holiday dinners.
Guests always ask for the recipe!*

20-oz. pkg. frozen peas
8-oz. can sliced water chestnuts,
  drained
4-oz. can sliced mushrooms,
  drained

10-3/4 oz. can cream of
  mushroom soup
1/4 c. milk
salt and pepper to taste

Mix together all ingredients in a large bowl; transfer to a lightly greased 2-quart casserole dish. Bake, uncovered, at 350 degrees for 30 minutes, or until bubbly and peas are tender. Serves 8.

Let kindness come with every gift and
good desires with every greeting.
– Robert Louis Stevenson

## Spinach Salad with Poppy Seed Dressing

*Jeanne Berfiend*
*Indianapolis, IN*

*Many years ago when I was a "young" wife, I was served this salad as part of our Proverbs 31 ministry by our elder ladies at church. It's festive and delicious year 'round. You may add sliced, grilled chicken, if you want to serve this as a main dish.*

6-oz. pkg. baby spinach, torn
1 pt. strawberries, hulled
   and sliced
1/2 c. red onion, chopped fine
1/2 c. chopped walnuts or pecans

In a large bowl, combine spinach, strawberries and onion. Just before serving time, divide among individual salad plates. Drizzle with Poppy Seed Dressing and sprinkle nuts on top. Serves 4.

### Poppy Seed Dressing:

1/2 c. mayonnaise-style
   salad dressing
1/4 c. sugar
2 T. poppy seed
2 T. white vinegar

Combine all ingredients in a jar; add lid and shake thoroughly.

Sugared nuts are delicious on salads! In a cast-iron skillet, combine one teaspoon butter, 1/4 cup sugar and 3/4 cup walnut or pecan halves. Cook and stir over medium heat for about 7 minutes, until sugar is golden and melted. Spread carefully on a greased baking sheet to cool.

# *Family-Pleasing Sides & Salads*

## Festive Cabbage Salad

*Mary Jo Klement*
*La Porte, IN*

*This salad looks so pretty on a holiday table.*
*People always ask for the recipe.*

14 c. red cabbage, shredded
1 c. chopped walnuts
1 c. dried cranberries
1/4 c. red onion, finely sliced

1/3 c. cider vinegar
1/3 c. oil
1/3 c. sugar
1 t. celery seed

In a large bowl, combine cabbage, walnuts, cranberries and onion; set aside. In a small bowl, whisk together remaining ingredients; add to cabbage mixture and toss. Cover and refrigerate overnight. Stir several times at serving time. Makes 8 to 10 servings.

Old-fashioned colored Christmas tree bulbs can spread cheer
even after they've ceased to glow. Simply arrange them in a
glass bowl for an easy centerpiece. Tuck in some
pine clippings for added cheer.

# Grandma's Best Christmas RECIPES

## Secret-Recipe Polish Cucumber Salad

*Kathy Kleman*
*Hales Corners, WI*

*This recipe has been in our family since 1972...it is made only at Christmas and occasionally at Easter. I have never seen anything like this recipe, so it's time to share it, so it can be enjoyed by all!*

1/2 c. sour cream
1/2 c. mayonnaise
2 t. cider vinegar
1 T. plus 1/4 t. dried dill weed
1/2 t. salt
1/2 c. green onions,
   finely chopped

1 English cucumber, finely
   chopped
1 head lettuce, halved and
   finely shredded

At least one day before serving, mix sour cream, mayonnaise, vinegar, dill weed and salt in a small bowl. Add onions; cover and refrigerate until serving time. (This allows flavors to blend.) About one hour before serving, prepare cucumber, blotting any excess moisture with a paper towel. Combine cucumber and lettuce in a large bowl. Let stand for 30 minutes to one hour. At serving time, spoon sour cream sauce over lettuce mixture. Fold in just enough to mix cucumber and lettuce; do not overmix. Transfer to a serving bowl and serve. Serves 8.

Begin a holiday journal...decorate a blank book, then use it to note each year's special moments, guests welcomed, meals shared, gifts given and received. You'll love looking back on these happy memories!

# Family-Pleasing Sides & Salads

## Surprise Salad

*Sandy Coffey*
*Cincinnati, OH*

*The sauerkraut is the surprise! This is a good one to serve*
*with roast pork for New Year's Day.*

2 c. sauerkraut, drained
 and rinsed
2 c. carrots, peeled and shredded
1 c. celery, chopped
1 c. green pepper, diced
1/2 c. onion, chopped
1/4 c. diced pimentos, drained
1/2 c. sugar
1/2 c. white vinegar
salt and pepper to taste

In a large bowl, mix together all ingredients. Cover and refrigerate at
least 4 hours before serving, up to one week. Stir again before serving.
Serves 4 to 6.

## Wanda's Vermicelli Salad

*Patty Stevens*
*Springhill, LA*

*At Howell Elementary School, our faculty had some great cooks.*
*Wanda was one of the best! For every occasion, her*
*vermicelli salad was requested.*

16-oz. pkg. vermicelli pasta,
 uncooked
4-oz. jar sliced pimentos, drained
 and finely chopped
4 to 5 stalks celery, chopped
3/4 c. onion, chopped
2 to 3 pickled jalapeño peppers,
 chopped, drained and
 2 T. juice reserved
3 to 4 c. mayonnaise
salt and pepper to taste

Cook pasta according to package directions; drain. Rinse in cold water;
drain and add to a large bowl. Add remaining ingredients including
reserved juice; stir together. Cover and refrigerate. Makes 10 to
12 servings.

## Potato Croquettes

*Nicoletta Amendola*
*Essex, CT*

*My aunt made these on holidays. I really don't know why she only made them on special days...I make them all the time! My family loves this recipe. Years ago when I made mashed potatoes, I would throw away the leftovers. Not anymore! You could also add bacon bits or diced, cooked ham or sausage to the mashed potato mixture. Don't try adding cheese...the cheese starts to melt! Makes a great side dish with any meat or fish dish.*

4 Idaho baking potatoes, peeled
   and quartered
butter and milk to taste
salt and pepper to taste

1 to 2 eggs, beaten
1/2 to 1 c. dry bread crumbs
1/3 c. olive oil for deep frying

In a saucepan, cover potatoes with water. Cook over medium-high heat until fork-tender; drain. Transfer potatoes to a large bowl. Mash potatoes, adding butter and milk as desired; season with salt and pepper. Cover and chill for several hours. (Potatoes must be cold, so don't skip this step.) With floured hands and working on a lightly floured surface, shape chilled potatoes into oval croquettes, 2 tablespoons per croquette. Dip croquettes into beaten egg; coat in bread crumbs. Add oil to a large deep saucepan; heat over medium-high heat. Working in batches, fry croquettes until golden on all sides. Drain on paper towels and serve. Serves 4.

Bring out Grandma's whimsical Christmas table linens for family gatherings. Decorated with smiling Santas or bright poinsettias, they're sure to spark fun memories.

# *Family-Pleasing Sides & Salads*

## Holiday Brussels Sprouts

*Gladys Kielar*
*Whitehouse, OH*

*These Brussels sprouts are special for holidays.*
*The recipe doubles easily for a larger group.*

16-oz. pkg. frozen Brussels
   sprouts
10-oz. pkg. frozen peas
2 T. butter

2 stalks celery, chopped
2 slices bacon, crisply cooked
   and crumbled
2 T. fresh chives, minced

Separately cook Brussels sprouts and peas according to package directions; drain. Meanwhile, in a large skillet, melt butter over medium-high heat. Add celery; cook and stir until crisp-tender. Add Brussels sprouts, peas, bacon and chives to skillet; toss to combine and heat through. Makes 6 servings.

Years ago, Christmas gifts were so much simpler. Recall those times with charming table favors. Fill brown paper sacks with a juicy orange, a popcorn ball, nuts to shell and old-fashioned hard candies. Tie with yarn and set one at each place, or heap in a basket. So sweet!

# Grandma's Best *Christmas* RECIPES

## Marsha's Butternut Squash Bake

*Marsha Baker*
*Palm Harbor, FL*

*I am asked to make this for every family meal with my children and grands. It is always a hit! Several years ago, I won a hundred dollars in a side-dish recipe contest with this recipe, and I'm always asked for it. It may be made ahead, but wait until you're ready to bake before adding the topping. I always double the topping recipe.*

1/3 c. butter, softened
2/3 c. sugar
2 eggs
5-oz. can evaporated milk

1 t. vanilla extract
2 c. butternut squash, peeled, cooked and mashed

Combine butter and sugar in a large bowl. Beat with an electric mixer on medium speed until blended. Beat in eggs, evaporated milk and vanilla. Stir in squash; mixture will be thin. Spread in a greased 11"x7" baking pan. Bake, uncovered, at 350 degrees for 45 minutes, or until almost set. Remove from oven; sprinkle with Topping. Return to oven for 5 to 10 minutes, until hot and bubbly. Makes 6 to 8 servings.

## Topping:

1/2 c. crispy rice cereal
1/4 c. chopped pecans

3 T. brown sugar, packed
2 T. butter, melted

Combine all ingredients; mix well.

Evaporated milk and sweetened condensed milk were both old standbys in Grandma's day. They're still handy today, but while they're both shelf-stable whole milk, they're not interchangeable, so double-check the recipe.

# Family-Pleasing Sides & Salads

## Dill & Chive Peas

JoAnn
Gooseberry Patch

*A simple, old-fashioned side...it reminds me of the peas
and herbs Great-Grandmother grew in her garden.*

14-oz. pkg. frozen baby peas
1 T. butter
1/4 c. fresh dill weed, snipped

2 T. fresh chives, minced
1 t. lemon pepper seasoning
1/4 t. salt

In a saucepan, cook peas according to package directions. Drain; stir in
remaining ingredients and serve. Serves 4.

## Sweet Onion Casserole

Cheri Maxwell
Gulf Breeze, FL

*My grandma always made this dish for our holiday dinners.*

4 T. butter, divided
2 to 3 sweet onions, sliced
10-3/4 oz. can cream of
   chicken soup

1/2 c. milk
1 t. soy sauce
8-oz. pkg. shredded Swiss cheese
1/2 loaf French bread, sliced

Melt 2 tablespoons butter in a large skillet over medium heat. Add
onions and sauté for 3 to 5 minutes, until crisp-tender. Transfer onions
to a lightly greased 12"x8" baking pan. In a bowl, whisk together
chicken soup, milk and soy sauce; spoon over onions. Sprinkle evenly
with cheese. Spread bread slices with remaining butter; arrange over
cheese. Bake, uncovered, at 350 degrees for 30 minutes, until bubbly
and bread is golden. Serves 8.

Grandma's secret...you'll shed fewer tears if you peel
an onion under cold running water.

## Jackie's Spring Mix Salad

*Donna Carter*
*Ontario, Canada*

*My good friend Jackie gave me this recipe years ago. This salad is so quick & easy to make. Great for get-togethers! For variety, sometimes I'll add some well-drained canned mandarin oranges, switch out pine nuts for sunflower seeds and goat cheese for feta cheese. Delicious, easy and oh-so good for you. Enjoy!*

6-oz. pkg. spring mix
  salad greens
5 to 6 cherry tomatoes, halved
1 English cucumber, sliced
1 yellow pepper, cubed
1 red onion, diced

1/3 c. dried cranberries
1/3 c. pine nuts
8-oz. bottle favorite vinaigrette
  salad dressing
2 T. crumbled feta cheese

In a large bowl, combine all ingredients except salad dressing and cheese; toss well. Cover and refrigerate until ready to serve. Just before serving, add salad dressing to taste and toss well. Sprinkle with cheese and serve. Makes 4 to 6 servings.

Grandmother never tossed out day-old bread and neither should you! It keeps its texture better than very fresh bread... it's thrifty too. Cut it into cubes, pack into freezer bags and freeze for making stuffing cubes, casserole toppings and herbed salad croutons.

# Family-Pleasing Sides & Salads

## Grandma's Secret Cranberry Relish

*Susan Sebrell*
*Youngstown, OH*

*When I was a child, my grandma kept this recipe a secret and refused to give it to anyone. But after I got married and began hosting the family holidays, then she gave it to me. I was very surprised to learn she used the whole orange, seeds, rind and all! But it's delicious. I have made this every Thanksgiving and Christmas get-together ever since. Great over turkey, ham and stuffing...it's what my family has done for many, many decades.*

12-oz. pkg. fresh cranberries
2 oranges, cut into small pieces,
   rind and all

2 3-oz. pkgs. cherry gelatin mix
1 c. sugar
1 c. water

Combine all ingredients in a blender. (May do half at a time.) Process to desired smoothness; transfer to a serving bowl. Cover and keep chilled. Freezes well; thaw in refrigerator overnight. (Do not refreeze.) Makes 4 cups.

For yummy-smelling, spiced pomanders, press whole cloves
into oranges, forming patterns or simply covering closely.
Roll in pumpkin pie spice or cinnamon. Stored in
a cool, dry place, they'll keep for years.

# Grandma's Best *Christmas* RECIPES

## Grandma's Perfect Potato Salad

*Kelly Thomas*
*Sarver, PA*

*My grandma, mom and I all used to make this potato salad for family holidays. They taught me how to cook, and I remember being in the kitchen as young as five years old. Now I am teaching my daughter these special recipes. When I'm expecting a smaller crowd, I cut this recipe in half and it works just as well.*

5 lbs. potatoes
6 eggs
1 lb. bacon, cut into small pieces
1 c. celery, chopped

1/2 c. onion, chopped
salt and pepper to taste
64-oz. jar mayonnaise

Add unpeeled potatoes to a large stockpot; cover with water. Bring to a boil over high heat; boil until fork-tender; drain. Peel potatoes and cube; place in a large bowl. At the same time, boil eggs in a saucepan of water for 12 to 14 minutes, until hard-boiled. Cook bacon in in a large skillet over medium heat until crisp; do not drain. Add entire contents of cooked bacon with drippings to potatoes in bowl. Peel eggs; dice and add to potatoes. Add celery, onion, salt and pepper. Add mayonnaise; mix thoroughly until creamy. Cover and refrigerate until chilled. May need to add more mayonnaise at serving time. Serves 12 to 14.

For a festive winter salad, drizzle spring mix greens with a quick & easy honey dressing. Whisk together 1/2 cup balsamic vinegar, 1/4 cup honey, 1/4 cup olive oil and one teaspoon soy sauce until smooth. Top salad with ruby-red pomegranate seeds and a toss of candied pecans...delicious!

# Family-Pleasing Sides & Salads

## Copper Pennies, or Marinated Carrots

*Lanita Anderson*
*Lake Lure, NC*

*My grandmother used to make this salad when I was growing up and it was on her table often, but especially for special occasions or holiday meals. It's easy to make, and brings back such good memories.*

1 lb. carrots, peeled and sliced
1/2 c. onion, chopped
1 green pepper, chopped
10-3/4 oz. can tomato soup

1/2 c. oil
1/2 c. white vinegar
1/2 c. sugar

In a saucepan, cover carrots with water. Boil over medium-high heat for 15 to 20 minutes, until crisp-tender; drain well and transfer to a bowl. Add onion and green pepper; set aside. Whisk together remaining ingredients in another saucepan; bring to a boil over medium-high heat. Remove from heat; spoon soup mixture over carrot mixture. Cover and refrigerate overnight before serving. Makes 6 servings.

Make some sweet and simple button wreaths. Choose buttons from Grandma's button box, or pick up a supply at a craft store. Simply thread large, flat buttons onto wire, then twist the ends to form a circle. Tie on a fluffy bow and hang on the Christmas tree.

# Grandma's Best Christmas
## RECIPES

## Potato-Leek Gratin

*Debbie Benzi*
*Binghamton, NY*

*We like this recipe because it's light-tasting, not heavy
with butter and cheese. Simmering the potatoes in the milk
cuts down on baking time.*

4 c. milk
1 clove garlic, minced
1 bay leaf
1 t. dried thyme
1 t. salt
1/4 t. pepper

3 lbs. potatoes, peeled and
   sliced 1/4-inch thick
2 c. leeks, thinly sliced
1 c. shredded Gruyère cheese,
   divided

In a Dutch oven, combine all ingredients except cheese. Bring to a
boil over medium-high heat. Reduce heat to medium-low; cover and
simmer for 10 minutes. Spoon half of potato mixture into a greased
13"x9" baking pan; sprinkle with half of cheese. Layer with remaining
potato mixture; sprinkle remaining cheese over all. Bake, uncovered, at
375 degrees for one hour, or until bubbly and golden. Discard bay leaf;
let stand 10 minutes before serving. Serves 6.

Leeks are delicious, but can be quite sandy when purchased. To
clean them easily, slice and soak in a bowl of cold water. Swish
them in the water and drain. Refill the bowl and swish again
until the water is clear. Drain again and pat dry.

# Family-Pleasing Sides & Salads

## Cheesy Corn Casserole

*Wendy Meadows*
*Spring Hill, FL*

*My husband's grandmother handed this recipe down to me a few months before she passed. She always made it when we would come visit because my son loved it. Sometimes I will add a can of mild green chiles to the mix to give a boost of flavor.*

8-1/2 oz. pkg. corn muffin mix
15-oz. can corn, drained
14-3/4 oz. can creamed corn
8-oz. container sour cream
1 c. shredded sharp Cheddar
   cheese
1/2 c. butter, melted

In a large bowl, combine dry corn muffin mix and remaining ingredients; mix well. Spread in a lightly greased 8"x8" baking pan. Bake, uncovered, at 350 degrees for 55 to 60 minutes, until set and golden. Serve hot or at room temperature. Makes 4 to 6 servings.

Grandma knew the best ways to keep kids entertained on snow days. Fill several squirt bottles with warm water and add a few drops of food coloring, then send the kids out to "paint" the snow...they'll love it!

# Grandma's Best *Christmas* RECIPES

## Gram's Holiday Broccoli

*Sandy Coffey*
*Cinncinnati, OH*

*A recipe I collected more than 20 years ago. It makes
a great addition to holiday dinners.*

1-1/2 to 2 lbs. broccoli,
  cut into spears
1 lemon, halved
10-3/4 oz. can cream of
  chicken soup

1/2 c. mayonnaise
2 T. butter, melted
1/4 t. curry powder
1/2 c. dry bread crumbs

Add broccoli spears to a saucepan of boiling water. Cook over medium
heat until fork-tender; drain. Arrange broccoli in a buttered 1-1/2 quart
casserole dish. Squeeze lemon halves over broccoli; set aside. Combine
remaining ingredients except bread crumbs in a bowl; mix well and
spoon over broccoli. Sprinkle with bread crumbs. Bake, uncovered,
at 350 degrees for 20 minutes, or until bubbly and golden. Makes
6 servings.

## Hearty Green Bean Casserole

*Christine Scott Olivieri*
*Norwich, CT*

*When my college and high school-age children came home for the
holidays, they loved this dish more than the roast turkey! It's a little
different, since it doesn't use the usual cream of mushroom soup.*

2  14-1/2 oz. cans French-cut
  green beans, drained
10-3/4 oz. can golden mushroom
  soup

12-oz. can evaporated milk
1/4 t. pepper
6-oz. can French fried onions,
  divided

In a large bowl, mix green beans and mushroom soup. Add
evaporated milk and pepper; blend well. Fold in onions, reserving
a few for garnish. Spread in a greased 2-quart casserole dish. Bake,
uncovered, at 350 degrees for 20 to 25 minutes. Arrange reserved
onions on top; bake for another 5 minutes. Let cool for 5 to 10 minutes
before serving. Serves 6 to 8.

# Family-Pleasing Sides & Salads

## Grandma's Creamed Spinach

*Paula Marchesi*
*Auburn, PA*

*I've made this side dish so often because it goes well with just about anything. Great with pasta or any meat, or mix it with leftover plain pasta for a meal in itself. It's one of our family's favorites.*

1 T. olive oil
1/2 c. onion, chopped
2  10-oz. pkgs. frozen chopped
   spinach, thawed and
   squeezed dry

2 cloves garlic, minced
8-oz. pkg. plain or onion & chive
   cream cheese, softened
1/4 c. 2% milk
salt and pepper to taste

Heat oil in a large skillet over medium-high heat. Add onion and cook until tender, stirring occasionally, 5 to 7 minutes. Add spinach and garlic; cook for 2 more minutes. Reduce heat to medium-low. Stir in remaining ingredients; cook and stir until cream cheese is melted. Serves 4.

Make mini wreaths of rosemary to slip around dinner napkins.
Simply wind fresh rosemary stems into a ring shape, tuck in
the ends and tie on a tiny bow...so festive!

## Carolyn's Spinach Waldorf Salad

*Carolyn Deckard
Bedford, IN*

*I love looking through my old recipes to find something
I haven't made for awhile. This salad looks so pretty
at Christmas, and it's delicious!*

1/2 c. mayonnaise
2 T. frozen apple juice
  concentrate, thawed
1/4 t. cinnamon
4 c. Red Delicious or Gala apples,
  cored and cubed

1/2 c. seedless red grapes, halved
1/2 c. celery, chopped
1/2 c. chopped walnuts
4 c. fresh spinach, torn

In a large bowl, combine mayonnaise, apple juice concentrate and
cinnamon; mix until well blended. Add apples, grapes, celery and
walnuts; stir to coat. Cover and refrigerate, if not serving right away.
At serving time, place spinach in a large salad bowl. Spoon apple
mixture over spinach; toss to mix and coat. Serves 8.

Start your own "Elf on the Shelf" tradition with the kids. Set out
a vintage elf figurine to "watch" for good behavior. Overnight, the
elf will report back to the North Pole (or so you tell the kids!).
Next morning, look for him sitting in a different spot. Such fun!

# *Family-Pleasing Sides & Salads*

## Cauliflower Salad

*Judy Phelan*
*Macomb, IL*

*My maternal grandmother made this scrumptious salad.*
*The recipe has been in the family over 50 years.*

1 head cauliflower, broken into
    small pieces
1 head lettuce, torn into
    small pieces
1/4 c. sweet onion, chopped

1/4 c. sugar
1 c. mayonnaise
1 lb. bacon, crisply cooked
    and crumbled
1 c. grated Parmesan cheese

In a large serving bowl, layer cauliflower, lettuce and onion; sprinkle sugar over all. Layer with mayonnaise, bacon and cheese. Cover and refrigerate overnight. At serving time, toss to mix well. Makes 8 to 10 servings.

Snowy paper-white narcissus flowers are a winter delight that
Grandma loved. Place paper-white bulbs in water-filled
bulb vases, pointed ends up. Set in a sunny window.
In about 6 weeks you'll have blooms!

## Layered Cranberry Salad

*Laurie Ellithorpe*
*Cambridge, NY*

*My grandmother made the best salads at holiday time.*
*This was one of my favorites...it still is!*

2 3-oz. pkgs. raspberry
   gelatin mix
1-1/2 c. boiling water
20-oz. can crushed pineapple
14-oz. can whole-berry
   cranberry sauce

3/4 c. cranberry juice, other fruit
   juice or water
1 c. toasted walnuts or pecans,
   chopped and divided

In a large bowl, combine gelatin mixes and boiling water. Stir for
2 minutes, or until completely dissolved. Add pineapple with juice,
cranberry sauce, cranberry juice and nuts, reserving a small amount of
nuts to sprinkle on top. Mix well; spoon into a 13"x9" glass baking pan.
Cover and refrigerate until firm, about 3 hours. Spread Cream Cheese
Topping over firm gelatin mixture; garnish with reserved nuts. Cover
and refrigerate for about one hour to allow the topping to firm up.
Serves 8 to 10.

## Cream Cheese Topping:

8-oz. pkg. cream cheese,
   softened

1/2 c. sugar
1 c. sour cream

In a large bowl, beat cream cheese and sugar with an electric mixer
on low to medium speed until well blended. Add sour cream and beat
until smooth.

Don't toss out that last bit of leftover cranberry sauce!
Purée it with balsamic vinaigrette to create a tangy
dressing for green salads.

# Family-Pleasing Sides & Salads

## Grandma Shearer's Green Salad

Cathy Shifley
Galion, OH

*My grandma made this salad for every holiday dinner. After she passed away, I made it as a joke for a family gathering, but the joke was on me! Everyone loved it and it became my required bring for get-togethers. It is also required at all church dinners; the minister's mother used to make it all the time, and he and his wife love it, too.*

3-oz. pkg. lemon gelatin mix
3-oz. pkg. lime gelatin mix
1-1/2 c. boiling water
1 c. small-curd cottage cheese
1/2 c. mayonnaise-style
   salad dressing

12-oz. can evaporated milk
20-oz. can crushed pineapple in
   juice, drained
10-oz. pkg. mini marshmallows

In a bowl, combine gelatin mixes and boiling water; stir for 2 minutes or until dissolved. Cover and put in freezer to cool. Meanwhile, in a large bowl, combine cottage cheese, salad dressing, evaporated milk and pineapple; mix well. Add cottage cheese mixture to cooled gelatin. Mix thoroughly and spoon into a 13"x9" glass baking pan. Spread marshmallows evenly over the top. Cover and refrigerate until set up, about 2 hours. Serves 10 to 12.

What good fortune to grow up in a home
where there are grandparents.
–Suzanne LaFollette

# Grandma's Best *Christmas* RECIPES

## Grandmother's Dressing & Gravy

*Tina Matie*
*Alma, GA*

*I have wonderful memories of going to my grandparents' home for the holidays. My grandmother would always have a tableful of good-smelling foods, but the one I remember the most was her dressing & gravy. She would always have two big pans made and it smelled so good! This recipe has been passed down in my family from generation to generation, and we still have this dish for the holidays. My grandmother always comes to mind when I make her dressing & gravy.*

8-1/2 oz. pkg. corn muffin mix
10 slices white bread
1/2 c. long-cooking grits, uncooked
2  14-1/2 oz. cans chicken or turkey broth

5 eggs, well beaten
1 t. onion powder
1 t. celery salt
1 t. salt
1 t. pepper

Bake corn muffin mix according to package directions. Toast bread slices until lightly golden. Cook grits according to package directions. Crumble cornbread and toasted bread into a large bowl; add cooked grits and set aside. In a saucepan over high heat, bring broth to a boil. Pour enough broth over bread mixture to moisten to a medium consistency. Cover bowl; allow to steam through. Add eggs and seasonings to bread mixture; mix well. Spoon mixture into a greased 13"x9" baking pan. Bake, uncovered, at 375 degrees for about 30 minutes, until hot and golden. Serve Gravy over dressing. Serves 15 to 20.

## Gravy:

10-3/4 oz. can cream of chicken soup
1 c. chicken or turkey broth

Optional: cooked turkey or chicken giblets, chopped

In a saucepan over medium heat, mix chicken soup and enough broth to thin to gravy consistency. Add giblets, if desired. Heat through.

# Family-Pleasing Sides & Salads

## Grandmother's Cranberry Relish

*Doug Shockley*
*Lincoln, NE*

*My grandma made this relish for both Thanksgiving and Christmas. You can make the recipe either tart or sweet...I really like it on the tart side. It can be frozen and served with pork chops or pork roast.*

2 to 3 12-oz. pkgs. fresh
   cranberries
1 Granny Smith apple, cored
   and quartered

1 navel orange, sectioned
zest of 1 orange
1/2 to 2 c. sugar, to taste

In a food processor or meat grinder, chop cranberries, apple and orange. Add orange zest and sugar; mix well. Cover and refrigerate for 24 hours or overnight. Makes 10 to 12 servings.

During the holidays, snap a photo of your family in the same place and same position each year...it will be a sweet reminder of how the kids have grown!

# Grandma's Best *Christmas* RECIPES

## Grandma Clarissa's Sweet Potatoes

*Vickie Wiseman*
*Liberty Twp., OH*

*My grandmother loved to combine cinnamon, nutmeg and cardamom in her recipes. If she was using one spice, she was usually using all three!*

2-1/2 lbs. sweet potatoes, peeled and quartered
1 T. butter
1/3 c. evaporated milk
1/4 c. brown sugar
1 t. vanilla extract
1 T. cinnamon
1-1/2 t. nutmeg
1 t. cardamom
10-oz. pkg. mini marshmallows

Cover sweet potatoes with water in a large saucepan. Cook over medium-high heat until fork-tender. Drain; transfer to a large bowl. Add remaining ingredients except marshmallows; beat until smooth. Spoon mashed sweet potatoes into a buttered 2-quart casserole dish; smooth the top with spoon. Sprinkle with additional spices, if desired; spread marshmallows on top. Cover with aluminum foil. Bake at 350 degrees for 20 minutes, or until hot and marshmallows are toasted. Makes 8 servings.

Repurpose holiday cards with this sweet idea. Trace a cookie-cutter shape around the main image of the card. Cut out the shape, punch a hole and tie to a pine garland with bright red ribbon or yarn.

# Family-Pleasing Sides & Salads

## Sautéed Garlic Asparagus with Bacon

*Ann Farris*
*Biscoe, AR*

*My dad started our asparagus bed over 20 years ago...*
*we still enjoy the asparagus that grows in it every year.*

1/2 lb. bacon, chopped
1 T. butter
3 cloves garlic, minced
1 t. Italian seasoning

salt and pepper to taste
2 lbs. asparagus, trimmed and
   cut into thirds

In a large skillet over medium-high heat, cook bacon until crisp. Set aside bacon on paper towels; drain skillet and wipe clean. Add remaining ingredients to skillet. Sauté over medium heat until tender, about 5 to 7 minutes. Return bacon to skillet and serve. Makes 6 to 8 servings.

## Spinach Custard

*Teresa Verell*
*Roanoke, VA*

*This old-fashioned spinach dish is excellent served*
*with steak, chicken or fish.*

4 eggs, beaten
1 c. whole milk
1/4 c. grated Parmesan cheese
1/4 t. nutmeg
1/4 t. sea salt

1/8 t. pepper
10-oz. pkg. frozen chopped
   spinach, thawed and
   squeezed dry

Combine all ingredients in a large bowl; beat well. Spoon into a greased 2-quart casserole dish. Bake, uncovered, at 350 degrees for 30 to 35 minutes, until set and a knife tip inserted midway between center and outer edge comes out clean. Let stand for 10 minutes before serving. Serves 4.

# Grandma's Best
# *Christmas*
## RECIPES

## Spiced Peaches

*Carmela Tallmeister*
*Ontario, Canada*

*I've made this recipe quite often at Christmas to accompany
roast pork, turkey, goose or duck. It is spicy, warming
and comforting on a cold winter's evening.*

2 c. water
4 4-inch cinnamon sticks
1 t. fresh ginger, peeled
    and minced
1 t. curry powder
1/2 t. allspice

1/2 t. nutmeg
4 15-1/4 oz. cans sliced peaches
    in syrup, drained and syrup
    reserved
1/4 t. salt

In a saucepan, combine water and spices. Simmer over medium heat for
20 minutes. Add reserved peach syrup; simmer for another 10 minutes.
Stir in salt; remove from heat and let cool. Add peaches to a large bowl;
pour warm liquid over peaches. Serve chilled or at room temperature.
Makes 6 servings.

## Nanny's Fruit Salad

*Kylee Lenhart*
*Sylvania, OH*

*This is one of the recipes my grandma would assign us to
bring to our family's Christmas night gathering. It's delicious!*

2 20-oz. cans pineapple chunks
    in juice, drained and 2 c. juice
    reserved
2 15-oz. cans mandarin oranges,
    drained

14-1/2 oz. jar maraschino
    cherries, drained
5 bananas, sliced
4.6-oz. box vanilla cook & serve
    pudding mix

Mix all fruits in a bowl; set aside. Prepare pudding mix according to
package directions, using reserved pineapple juice instead of water. Cook
until thickened; remove from heat and let cool for about 20 minutes.
Pour over fruits; stir gently. Cover and refrigerate until ready to serve.
Makes 8 servings.

# Snowy-Day Soups & Breads

## Cozy Chicken & Cheese Soup

*Amanda Spears-Allen*
*Decatur, AL*

*When I was a child, my granny and I would curl up on Friday evenings with big bowls full of this warm, filling soup while watching reruns of* Little House on the Prairie *together. Serve with your choice of biscuits, cornbread or crackers...yummy!*

2 boneless, skinless chicken
  breasts
2 c. broccoli, chopped
2 c. carrots, peeled and
  thinly sliced
10-3/4 oz. can cream of
  onion soup

8-oz. container half-and-half
2 5-1/2 oz. pkgs. chicken &
  broccoli rice mix
1 t. garlic, minced
salt and pepper to taste
8-oz. pkg. sharp Cheddar
  cheese, diced

In a large saucepan, cover chicken breasts with water. Simmer over medium heat until chicken is tender. Remove chicken to a plate; cool and refrigerate. Reserve 2 cups broth from pan. In a 6-quart slow cooker, combine reserved chicken broth, broccoli and carrots. Cover and cook on high setting for 4 hours. Dice chicken and add to slow cooker along with remaining ingredients; mix gently. Cover and cook on low setting for one hour, stirring every 15 to 20 minutes, or until rice is tender. Stir again and serve. Makes 6 to 8 servings.

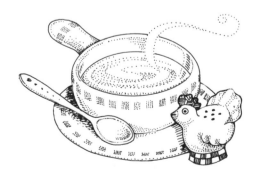

For juicy, flavorful chicken, cover with water and simmer
gently until cooked through, then turn off the heat
and let the chicken cool in its own broth.

# Snowy-Day Soups & Breads

## Cream of Broccoli Soup

*Lisa Gowen*
*St. Charles, MO*

*My girlfriend brought this delicious yummy soup to a get-together.
I just had to have this wonderful recipe. I thought it would be
complicated, but it's not! You can have this ready to serve in
30 minutes. Serve with warm crusty bread.*

2 large bunches broccoli,
   chopped
4 c. half-and-half
2 10-3/4 oz. cans cream of
   onion soup

2 10-3/4 oz. cans cream of
   celery soup
16-oz. pkg. pasteurized process
   cheese, cubed

Add broccoli to a large saucepan of boiling water. Cook until tender;
drain and set aside. In a large soup pot, combine remaining ingredients;
stir well. Cook over medium-low heat, stirring constantly, until cheese
is melted. Stir in broccoli and serve. Makes 6 servings.

## Ranch Oyster Crackers

*Vickie Wiseman*
*Liberty Twp., OH*

*These crackers have a nice flavor...my grandchildren love to
eat them by the handfuls! They are great to put in baggies
and take as a snack when traveling as well.*

16-oz. pkg. oyster crackers
1/2 to 3/4 c. salad oil
1-oz. pkg. buttermilk ranch
   salad dressing mix

1 t. dried dill weed
1/4 t. lemon pepper
1/4 t. garlic powder

Spread crackers on an ungreased large rimmed baking sheet; set aside.
Combine remaining ingredients in a bowl; mix well and spoon over
crackers. Stir to coat. Bake at 250 degrees for 15 to 20 minutes; cool.
Store up to 4 weeks in a tightly covered container. Makes 8 servings.

# Grandma's Best *Christmas* RECIPES

## Dill Pickle Potato Soup

*Tiffany Jones*
*Batesville, AR*

*One winter day, our area was experiencing sleet and freezing rain.
I was in the mood for some warm, comforting soup. I had seen a
similar recipe but didn't have all the ingredients. My version was
amazing...so delicious!*

1 T. olive oil
1 onion, diced
2 T. all-purpose flour
2 14-oz. cans vegetable broth
7 potatoes, peeled and cubed
14-1/2 oz. can sliced carrots,
    drained

salt and pepper to taste
2 c. dill pickle juice
5 large dill pickles, chopped
1/2 c. whipping cream
Optional: spicy jalapeño-flavored
    cream cheese, bacon bits

Heat oil in a large soup pot over medium-high heat. Add onion and
sauté until tender. Add flour; cook and stir until onion is coated. Add
vegetable broth, potatoes, carrots, salt and pepper; bring to a boil. Reduce
heat to medium; simmer until potatoes are fork-tender. Stir in pickle
juice, pickles and cream; continue cooking until heated through. If
desired, add a dollop of cream cheese to individual bowls; ladle in soup.
Stir to melt the cream cheese and top with bacon bits. Makes 6 servings.

Spread out cotton batting as a snowy setting for tiny vintage
houses and reindeer or snowman figures...what a sweet
centerpiece! Add a dash of mica flakes for icy sparkle.

# Snowy-Day Soups & Breads

## Irish Soda Bread

*Arlene Costello*
*Daytona Beach Shores, FL*

*My mother, Agnes Brady, who died 35 years ago, was born in Belfast, Ireland. She gave me this recipe for Irish soda bread. I have always made her soda bread, and it is always well received by family & friends. It keeps well and also freezes well.*

| | |
|---|---|
| 4 c. all-purpose flour | 1/2 t. salt |
| 1 c. sugar | 3 eggs, beaten |
| 2 t. baking powder | 16-oz. container sour cream |
| 1 t. baking soda | 1 c. raisins or dried cranberries |

In a large bowl, combine flour, sugar, baking powder, baking soda and salt; mix well. Add eggs, sour cream and raisins or cranberries; stir until just combined. Batter will be thick. Divide batter evenly between 2 greased 8"x4" loaf pans. Bake at 325 degrees for one hour. Makes 2 loaves.

Uncles and aunts, and cousins, are all very well,
and fathers and mothers are not to be despised;
but a grandmother, at holiday time,
is worth them all.

–Fanny Fern

## Chicken Tortilla Soup

*Elizabeth Smithson*
*Mayfield, KY*

*My granddaughter's favorite! I have to make it for her whenever she comes to visit. I use roast chicken from the deli.*

1/4 c. butter
1/2 c. onion, chopped
2 T. all-purpose flour
2 c. chicken broth
2 boneless, skinless chicken breasts, cooked and cubed or shredded
15-1/2 oz. can kidney beans, drained

15-1/2 oz. can black beans, drained
15-oz. can corn, drained
1-oz. pkg. taco seasoning mix
2 t. ground cumin
2 c. whipping cream
Garnish: shredded Pepper Jack Cheese, tortilla chips

Melt butter in a skillet over medium heat; add onion and cook until soft. Sprinkle flour over skillet; cook and stir until thickened and golden. Stir in remaining ingredients except cream and garnish; simmer for 15 to 20 minutes. Shortly before serving, stir in cream and heat through. Ladle into bowls; serve topped with cheese, with tortilla chips for dipping. Makes 4 to 6 servings.

Host a caroling party! Gather up friends and serenade the neighbors, or the residents of a nearby care home. Back home, have slow cookers waiting, filled with yummy soup and a hot beverage ready to warm everyone up. A sweet way to welcome the holiday.

# Snowy-Day Soups & Breads

## Corn & Potato Chowder

*Lisanne Miller*
*Wells, ME*

*This soup is wonderful in the wintertime...warms you all over on a cold evening. Serve with warm French bread and butter.*

3 slices bacon, crisply cooked
  and crumbled
1-1/4 c. potatoes, peeled
  and diced
1/4 c. onion, diced

15-oz. can corn, drained
14-3/4 oz. can creamed corn
1-1/2 c. chicken broth
pepper to taste
3/4 c. milk or whipping cream

Combine all ingredients except milk or cream in a 4-quart slow cooker. Cover and cook on low setting for 7 to 9 hours. Stir in milk or cream; cover and cook for 45 minutes longer. Serves 4 to 6.

## Pammy's Easy Batter Rolls

*Carolyn Deckard*
*Bedford, IN*

*The first thing our dinner guests ask my daughter is, did she bring her famous dinner rolls? They are so light, airy and irresistibly delicious. She has to double her recipe for our big family.*

3 c. all-purpose flour, divided
2 T. sugar
1 env. active dry yeast
1 t. salt

1 c. water
2 T. butter, sliced
1 egg
Garnish: melted butter

In a large bowl, combine 2 cups flour, sugar, yeast and salt; set aside. Combine water and butter in a saucepan over high heat; heat to 120 to 130 degrees. Add hot water to flour mixture; beat with a mixer on low speed until blended. Add egg; beat on low speed for 30 seconds, then on high speed for 3 minutes. Stir in remaining flour. Batter will be stiff; do not knead. Cover and let rise in a warm place until double, about 30 minutes. Stir dough down. Divide dough among 12 greased muffin cups, filling 1/2 full. Cover and let rise until double, about 15 minutes. Bake at 350 degrees for 15 to 20 minutes, until golden. Cool in pan for one minute; remove rolls to a wire rack. Brush tops with melted butter. Makes one dozen.

# Grandma's Best *Christmas* RECIPES

## Warm-You-Up Bean Chili

*Cindy Slawski*
*Medford Lakes, NJ*

*This scrumptious meatless chili is great for warming up after making a snowman or taking a walk through the neighborhood to look at Christmas lights! It tastes even better the next day.*

1 T. olive oil
2 c. onion, chopped
3 cloves garlic, minced
4 c. water, divided
2 14-1/2 oz. cans diced tomatoes
15-oz. can chickpeas, drained
   and rinsed
15-1/2 oz. can black beans,
   drained and rinsed
15-1/2 oz. can kidney beans,
   drained and rinsed
15-1/2 oz. can white beans,
   drained and rinsed
2 T. sugar
2 T. chili powder, or to taste
2 T. Worcestershire sauce
6-oz. can tomato paste
Garnish: shredded Cheddar or
   Mexican cheese

Heat oil in a large soup pot over medium-high heat. Add onion and garlic; sauté for 3 minutes, or until tender. Add 3 cups water, tomatoes with juice and remaining ingredients except tomato paste and garnish. Stir to combine. Combine tomato paste and remaining water in a small bowl; whisk until blended and stir into soup. Bring to a boil over medium-high heat. reduce heat to medium-low. Simmer for 15 to 20 minutes, stirring occasionally, until heated through. Top individual bowls of soup with cheese and serve. Makes 8 servings.

Have the kids build a snowman at an older neighbor's house while she's out shopping... won't she be delighted!

## Buttermilk Cornbread

*Ann Farris*
*Biscoe, AR*

*This recipe has been passed down in my family from grandmother, to mother, to children and grandchildren. The main rule to making cornbread in our family...it must be made in a well-seasoned cast-iron skillet. No other pan will live up to our cornbread!*

1 T. bacon drippings
1/2 c. butter
2 eggs, beaten
1/8 t. sugar
1 c. buttermilk

1/2 t. baking soda
1 c. white cornmeal
1 c. all-purpose flour
1/2 t. salt

Add bacon drippings and butter to a cast-iron skillet; set pan in 375-degree oven to heat. Meanwhile, beat eggs in a large bowl; stir in sugar. Combine buttermilk and baking soda in a small bowl; stir into egg mixture. Add cornmeal, flour and salt; stir until blended and few lumps remain. Carefully remove hot skillet from oven; pour batter into skillet. Bake at 375 degrees for 30 to 40 minutes, until a toothpick inserted in the center comes out clean. Cut into wedges and serve. Makes 6 servings.

Greet guests with a vintage sled next to the front door.
Tie on a pair of ice skates, or dress it up with
greenery, holly and pine cones.

# Grandma's Best *Christmas* RECIPES

## Mom's Ham & Bean Soup

*Sandra Turner*
*Fayetteville, NC*

*My mother cooked wonderful meals for our family every day. When the weather turned cooler, she made this delicious soup...it warmed us up, inside and out. It's a great recipe to use with the leftover ham bone after the holidays.*

1 meaty ham bone
10 c. water
1 large carrot, peeled and grated
1 large potato, peeled and grated
1/2 c. onion, diced
1/2 c. celery, diced
2 to 3  15.8-oz. cans Great
    Northern or navy beans,
    drained and rinsed

15-oz. can tomato sauce
1 t. Worcestershire sauce
1/2 t. seasoned salt
1/2 t. salt
1/2 t. pepper

In a large soup pot, combine ham bone, water, carrot, potato, onion and celery. Bring to a boil over high heat; reduce heat to medium-low. Simmer for about one hour, until vegetable mixture is tender and ham is coming off the bone. Remove bone and allow to cool; cut off ham and add to soup pot. Stir in beans, sauces and seasonings; simmer until heated through. Makes 6 servings.

Why not get out Grandma's soup tureen set for cozy soup dinners? The lid keeps soup piping hot and steamy, while the ladle makes serving easy.

## Chicken Gnocchi Soup

*Connie Litfin*
*Carrollton, TX*

*This is a recipe that I kept changing until we thought it had enough flavor. It's delicious...great the next day, too.*

3 T. butter
1 T. olive oil
1 c. onion, chopped
1/2 c. celery, chopped
1/4 c. all-purpose flour
1 T. dried parsley
1 t. granulated garlic
1/4 t. pepper
2 c. half-and-half

2 14-oz. cans chicken broth
5-1/2 oz. pkg. baby spinach, chopped
1 c. carrots, peeled and shredded
1-1/2 to 2 c. cooked chicken breast, chopped
16-oz. pkg. potato gnocchi pasta, uncooked

In a large soup pot over medium-high heat, melt butter with olive oil. Add onion and celery; sauté for several minutes, until tender. Add flour and cook for one minute, stirring constantly. Stir in parsley, garlic and pepper. Slowly stir in half-and-half and broth; add remaining ingredients. Simmer over medium heat, stirring occasionally, until gnocchi is tender and soup is thickened. Makes 6 to 8 servings.

Crunchy bread sticks are tasty soup dippers. Stand them up in a colorful snack pail... they'll take up little space on a soup buffet.

## Classic Beef Vegetable Soup

*Deanna Adams*
*Garland, TX*

*This soup is a perennial favorite! We celebrate our family Christmas on Christmas Eve. My mother began a tradition of soup for dinner and everyone's favorite snacks, like cheeses, meats and chips & dips...then the presents! Afterwards, we always had Christmas cookies and ice cream for dessert.*

2 to 3 T. oil
3-lb. beef chuck roast
2 white or yellow onions,
   cut into 1/2-inch cubes
2 T. tomato paste
4 stalks celery, cut into 1/2-inch
   cubes
4 carrots, peeled and cut
   into 1/2-inch cubes

28-oz. can stewed tomatoes
2 32-oz. containers beef broth
3 bay leaves
salt and pepper to taste
4 russet potatoes, peeled
   and cubed
16-oz. pkg. frozen mixed
   vegetables

In an 8-quart stockpot, heat oil over medium-high heat until a drop of water sizzles. Add roast; brown roast on both sides and remove to a plate. Reduce heat to medium and add onions; sauté until translucent or lightly golden. Push onions to sides of pan. Add tomato paste to center of pan; cook until just fragrant and stir to combine with onions. Add celery, carrots, tomatoes with juice and beef broth; return roast to pan. Add bay leaves around roast. Add water to fill pan about one to 2 inches below the rim. Season with salt and pepper. Bring to a boil; reduce heat to medium-low. Cover and simmer for 2 hours. Remove roast to a plate; shred and return to pan, discarding bones and any excess fat. Add potatoes and mixed vegetables; simmer an additional 20 minutes, or until potatoes are tender. Remove bay leaves; add additional salt and pepper as needed and serve. Serves 8 to 12.

Try a jar of chicken or beef soup base next time you cook up a pot of soup. It's a paste-like product that adds extra-rich homemade flavor to soups. Easy to store too...one jar in the fridge can replace a whole shelf of canned broth.

# Snowy-Day Soups & Breads

## Baked Potato Soup

*Elizabeth Smithson*
*Mayfield, KY*

*I always come back to this recipe for potato soup...it's an all-time best! I've had it for years, and it is always good.*

2 baking potatoes, peeled
   and cubed
1/3 c. butter
1/3 c. all-purpose flour
3-1/2 to 4 c. evaporated milk

2 green onions, chopped
1 c. shredded Cheddar cheese
3/4 c. real bacon bits
1/2 c. sour cream
salt and pepper to taste

In a saucepan, cover potatoes with water. Cook over medium-high heat until tender; drain and set aside. In another saucepan, melt butter over medium heat. Stir in flour; cook and stir until smooth and golden. Gradually add evaporated milk; cook and stir until thickened. Add cooked potatoes and onions; bring to a boil, stirring constantly. Reduce heat to medium-low; simmer until potatoes are very soft. Add remaining ingredients; cook and stir until cheese is melted. If too thick, add a little water. Serve immediately. Serves 4.

## Old-Fashioned Drop Biscuits

*Sandy Coffey*
*Cincinnati, OH*

*These light and fluffy biscuits are so good with meals. Spread with butter and jelly or apple butter...yum!*

1-3/4 c. all-purpose flour
1/4 c. cornstarch
4 t. baking powder

1 t. salt
1/4 c. oil
3/4 c. milk

In a large bowl, mix together flour, cornstarch, baking powder and salt. Add oil and milk; stir lightly. Drop batter by teaspoonfuls onto an oiled baking sheet. Bake at 450 degrees for 12 to 15 minutes, until golden. Makes about one dozen.

## New England Clam Chowder

*Linda Graff*
*Powell, WY*

*My sister-in-law gave us this recipe more than 30 years ago, and we've been serving this delicious chowder on Christmas Eve ever since. We love it because it is so thick and creamy. It has always been a hit with guests, too!*

1 c. potatoes, peeled and
    finely chopped
1 c. onion, finely chopped
1 c. celery, finely chopped
3 to 4 6-1/2 oz. cans minced
    clams, drained and
    juice reserved
3/4 c. butter

3/4 c. all-purpose flour
4 c. half-and-half or
    whipping cream
1 T. red wine vinegar
1 to 1-1/2 t. salt
1/16 t. white pepper
Garnish: real bacon bits

Combine potatoes, onion and celery in a large saucepan. Pour reserved clam juice over vegetable mixture in pan; add enough water to barely cover vegetables. Simmer over medium heat until vegetables are barely tender; do not drain. Meanwhile, melt butter in a soup pot over medium heat. Add flour and cook, stirring constantly, until well blended. Add half-and-half or cream; stir with a whisk until very thick. Add undrained vegetable mixture, clams, vinegar, salt and pepper; stir. Simmer until heated through. Serve with bacon bits on the side. Serves 6 to 8.

Crisp, savory crackers are delightful alongside steamy bowls of soup. Spread saltines with softened butter and sprinkle with Italian seasoning and garlic powder. Bake at 350 degrees for just a few minutes, until golden.

# Snowy-Day Soups & Breads

## Ski Lodge Oyster Bisque

*Teresa Verell*
*Roanoke, VA*

*This recipe is always requested after a day of snow skiing.*
*Serve with plenty of oyster crackers. Use the best butter and enjoy!*

4  10-oz. cans oyster stew
7 c. whole milk
1 c. water

1/2 c. butter, sliced
1/8 t. ground mace
1/8 t. pepper

Combine all ingredients in a large stockpot; stir until well mixed. Bring to a boil over high heat, stirring occasionally. Reduce heat to medium-low. Simmer for 10 minutes, stirring occasionally. Serve immediately. Makes 5 servings.

## Creamy Tomato Bisque

*Vickie*
*Gooseberry Patch*

*In the wintertime, there's nothing better than a cup of hot tomato*
*bisque after an afternoon spent outdoors! This is easy and good.*

1 T. olive oil
1 c. onion, diced
2 cloves garlic, minced
32-oz. container chicken broth

28-oz. can crushed tomatoes
2 T. tomato paste
1/2 c. whipping cream
salt and pepper to taste

Heat oil in a soup pot over medium-high heat. Cook onion for several minutes, until softened. Add garlic; cook for another minute. Stir in chicken broth, tomatoes with juice and tomato paste. Reduce heat to medium-low. Simmer for 30 minutes to one hour, stirring occasionally. Process soup to desired consistency with an immersion blender. Stir in cream; heat through, but do not boil. Season with salt and pepper. Serves 8.

A swirl of cream and a sprinkling of herbs makes any bowl of cream soup special for company.

# Grandma's Best *Christmas* RECIPES

## Creamy Mushroom Soup

*Lisa McClelland*
*Columbus, OH*

*This savory, warming soup often began our holiday meals.*
*My grandma was known as an excellent cook, so the family*
*gathered at her home during the holidays. Sweet memories!*

2 c. yellow onions, chopped
1/4 c. butter, divided
1-3/4 c. sliced mushrooms
2 t. garlic, minced
1/8 t. salt
2 t. dried dill weed, divided
2 c. chicken broth, divided
1 T. sweet Hungarian paprika

1 T. soy sauce
Optional: 1/4 c. white wine
3 T. all-purpose flour
1 c. milk
sea salt and pepper to taste
1/2 c. sour cream
Garnish: chopped fresh parsley

In a skillet over medium heat, sauté onions in 2 tablespoons butter until translucent. Add mushrooms, garlic, salt and one teaspoon dill weed. Stir in 1/2 cup chicken broth, paprika, soy sauce and wine, if using. Cover and simmer over low heat for 15 minutes. Melt remaining butter in a large saucepan over medium heat. Whisk in flour; cook and whisk for about 5 minutes. Stir in milk. Cook and stir over low heat, taking care not to let it scorch, for 10 minutes or until thickened. Stir in mushroom mixture and remaining broth. Cover and simmer for 10 to 15 minutes. Just before serving, season with salt and pepper; stir in sour cream and remaining dill weed. Serve garnished with parsley. Serves 4.

On a visit to the Christmas tree farm, tote along a vintage
thermos filled with hot soup...it'll really hit the spot!
Before ladling in the soup, fill the thermos with hot
water for 10 minutes to prewarm it.

# Snowy-Day Soups & Breads

## Turkey & Butternut Squash Soup

*Marcia Marcoux*
*Charlton, MA*

*Easy to make and very hearty! Garnish with
a swirl of cream, if you like.*

2 to 3 slices bacon, chopped
1 lb. ground turkey
32-oz. container butternut
   squash soup
15-1/2 oz. can red kidney beans,
   drained

1/2 c. sun-dried tomatoes, sliced
1 T. tomato paste
1 c. water
1/2 t. allspice
salt and pepper to taste

Cook bacon in a soup pot over medium heat until crisp; set aside on
paper towels. In the same skillet, cook turkey until browned; drain,
if needed. Stir in bacon and remaining ingredients. Simmer for 15 to
20 minutes; stir again and serve. Makes 4 to 6 servings.

## Pumpkin Provolone Corn Muffins

*Courtney Stultz*
*Weir, KS*

*Cornbread is a must with chili...but sometimes, we like to switch
things up! The combination of pumpkin and provolone cheese in this
recipe is delicious. Top with butter, if desired.*

1-1/2 c. all-purpose flour
1-1/4 c. cornmeal
2 t. baking powder
1/2 t. sea salt
2 t. smoked paprika
1/2 t. garlic powder

1/2 c. canned pumpkin
1 c. shredded provolone cheese
2 eggs, beaten
2 T. olive oil
1 c. milk

In a large bowl, mix together flour, cornmeal, baking powder, salt and
seasonings. Add remaining ingredients; stir just until combined. Spoon
into 12 greased or paper-lined muffin cups. Bake at 350 degrees for
18 to 20 minutes, until lightly golden and set. Let cool about 5 minutes
before serving. Makes one dozen.

# Grandma's Best *Christmas* RECIPES

## Mom's Cream of Chicken & Rice Soup

*Spencer Britt*
*Montgomery, IL*

*This recipe was my mother's go-to for cream of chicken & rice soup, and it's still a family favorite. She has since passed, but I have taken up the mantle to continue to make this delicious soup for the family during cold weather months, or any time anybody is in need of a hearty bowl of chicken soup. There is nothing like a food memory to warm the heart!*

1/4 c. butter
1 yellow onion, chopped
3 stalks celery, chopped
1 to 2 carrots, peeled and
    shredded or sliced
1/2 c. all-purpose flour
8 c. salt-free chicken broth
3 c. cooked white rice

1 to 2 c. cooked chicken,
    cubed or shredded
1/4 t. salt
1/4 t. pepper
12-oz. can evaporated milk
Garnish: chopped fresh chives
    or parsley

Melt butter in a large stockpot over medium heat. Sauté onion, celery and carrots until tender and onion is translucent. Sprinkle with flour; stir until combined. Continue cooking for 2 to 3 minutes. Gradually add chicken broth, 1/2 to one cup at a time, stirring to avoid lumps, until all broth has been added. Stir in rice, chicken, salt and pepper. Bring to a boil; reduce heat to medium-low. Simmer for about 10 minutes. Stir in evaporated milk; continue cooking another 3 to 5 minutes. Garnish with fresh herbs as desired. Makes 8 servings.

Pull out oversize coffee mugs when serving soups. They're just right for sharing hearty servings, and the handles make them so easy to hold onto. Great for warming chilly hands, too!

# Snowy-Day Soups & Breads

## Sue's Southern Fruit Bread

*Tish Dersnah*
*Saline, MI*

*Many years ago, we had a woman's book group at our church. We never got around to talking about the books, but we did enjoy our desserts! When our friend Sue served this bread, we couldn't get enough of it. I make it every Christmas. The recipe makes one lovely loaf, also good for gifting.*

3/4 c. all-purpose flour
1/4 t. baking powder
1/4 t. baking soda
2 c. whole pitted dates
1-1/2 c. pitted dried apricots
3 c. walnut and/or pecan halves
3/4 c. brown sugar, packed
3 eggs, beaten
1 t. vanilla extract

In a large bowl, combine flour, baking powder and baking soda; mix well. In another bowl, mix together fruits, nuts and brown sugar; add to flour mixture and set aside. In a small bowl, beat eggs with vanilla; add to batter and mix well. Batter will be thick and chunky, so use your hands if necessary to make sure it is mixed well. Pack batter into a greased 9"x5" loaf pan. Bake at 300 degrees for 1-1/2 hours. Cool on a wire rack; turn out of pan. Makes one loaf.

A loaf of homemade fruit bread is always a welcome gift! Make sure it stays fresh and tasty...let the bread cool completely before wrapping well in plastic wrap or aluminum foil.

## Cheesy Potato-Bacon Soup

*Toni Groves*
*Walshville, IL*

*My husband doesn't usually care for potato soup, but he eats this
and says it is good. The recipe makes plenty for a crowd.*

6 slices bacon, diced
2 c. chicken broth
8 potatoes, peeled and cubed
1 carrot, peeled and grated
1/2 c. onion, chopped
1 T. dried parsley
1/2 t. celery seed

1/2 t. salt
1/2 t. pepper
3 c. half-and-half
3 T. all-purpose flour
8-oz. pkg. pasteurized process
   cubed

In a large saucepan over medium heat, cook bacon until crisp; drain,
returning bacon to pan. Add chicken broth, potatoes, carrot, onion,
parsley, celery seed, salt and pepper. Cover and simmer until potatoes
are tender. Combine half-and-half and flour in a covered container;
shake until smooth and add to soup. Bring to a boil; boil for 2 minutes,
stirring constantly. Add cheese; stir until melted and serve. Serves 8
to 10.

Don't miss out on the season's first swirling snowflakes! Bundle
up the family and go on a winter hike, or take everyone to
a garden center or historic village where horse-drawn carriage
rides are given. Afterwards, warm everyone up with mugs
of hot soup...what memories!

# Snowy-Day Soups & Breads

## Cheddar Ham Chowder

*Gloria Schantz*
*Zionsville, PA*

*Delicious! This chowder is very good...it's a real keeper.*

2 c. water
2 c. potatoes, peeled and sliced
1/2 c. carrots, peeled and sliced
1/2 c. celery, sliced
1/4 c. onion, chopped
1 t. salt
1/4 t. pepper

1/4 c. butter
1/4 c. all-purpose flour
2 c. whole milk
8-oz. pkg. shredded Cheddar
   cheese
15-1/4 oz. can corn, drained
1-1/2 c. cooked ham, cubed

In a large saucepan over medium heat, combine water, potatoes, carrots, celery, onion, salt and pepper. Bring to a boil; reduce heat to medium-low. Cover and simmer for 8 to 10 minutes, until vegetables are tender. Remove from heat; do not drain. Meanwhile, in another saucepan, melt butter over medium heat; stir in flour. Gradually stir in milk. Cook until thick and bubbly, stirring often. Add cheese and stir until melted. Add milk mixture to undrained vegetable mixture. Stir in corn and ham; heat through. Makes 6 to 8 servings.

No fireplace? Hang stockings from stair railings, doorknobs, bookshelves or the backs of chairs!

# Grandma's Best Christmas RECIPES

## Grandma Lola's Vegetable Soup for a Crowd

*Barbara Cooper*
*Orion, IL*

*I have had this soup every Christmas Eve since becoming part of the family I married into...49 years and counting! Lola is no longer with us, but the soup is a tradition I'm happy to continue. This recipe is easy to cut in half and also easy to freeze. It always tastes better the next day, so I usually make mine on December 23rd. One year, I made it early in December and froze it in ice cream buckets...warmed up, it was just as good as always!*

2 3-lb. beef chuck roasts
4 c. water, divided
2 1.35-oz. pkgs. onion soup mix
3-1/2 c. canned diced tomatoes
10-oz. pkg. frozen whole
   green beans
2 c. frozen corn
2 c. russet potatoes, peeled
   and cubed
1 c. yellow onions, chopped
1-1/2 c. carrots, peeled and sliced

1 c. celery, chopped
6-oz. can tomato paste
1 T. sugar
2 t. dried parsley
4 32-oz. containers beef broth,
   or more as needed
salt and pepper to taste
2 c. cabbage, thickly sliced
Optional: 2/3 c. pearled barley,
   uncooked

Place roasts in a 6-quart slow cooker; set aside. In a saucepan, stir together 3 cups water and onion soup mixes. Bring to a boil over high heat; pour over roasts. Cover and cook on high setting for 8 hours or overnight. In the morning, remove roasts to a platter; let cool and shred. Cover and refrigerate beef. Reserve juices in slow cooker; strain. Add to a very large soup pot with remaining ingredients except cooked beef, cabbage and optional barley. Bring to a boil over medium-high heat; reduce heat to medium-low and simmer for 2 hours. Add beef, cabbage and barley, if using. Simmer for one more hour, or until vegetables are tender-crisp, not mushy. Serves 25.

If guests will be arriving at different times, keep soup simmering in a slow cooker set on low.

# Snowy-Day Soups & Breads

## Grandma Fayma's Bread

*Donna Hibbard*
*Yates Center, KS*

*A family favorite always made by my paternal grandma. She could make it the best! This dough can be made into 7 or 8 loaves of bread, or into 2 dozen wonderful cinnamon rolls. If you don't need this much bread, be a blessing and share!*

5 c. very warm water, about
   110 to 115 degrees
3 T. active dry yeast
2 eggs, beaten
1 c. sugar

1 c. shortening, warmed
1/4 c. salt
5 lbs. all-purpose flour,
   or as needed
Garnish: softened butter

In a large bowl, mix warm water and yeast; let stand for 5 minutes. In a very large bowl, stir together eggs, sugar, shortening and salt; add yeast mixture and mix well. Stir in flour until moistened; this may take most of the flour. Turn out dough onto a floured surface. Knead until dough is firm and not sticky, adding more flour, if needed. Return dough to bowl; cover and let rise until double in size. Turn out dough and knead again. Form dough into 7 to 8 loaves; place each in a greased 9"x5" loaf pan. Cover and let rise again in a warm area. Bake 2 to 3 loaves at a time. Bake at 375 degrees for 25 to 30 minutes, until golden. Brush with butter while still warm. Makes 7 to 8 loaves, or one loaf and 2 dozen rolls.

## Cinnamon Rolls:

Divide dough in half. For each half, roll out 1/2-inch thick on a floured surface. Brush with 1/2 cup melted butter; sprinkle generously with brown sugar and cinnamon. Roll up; slice one-inch thick. Place rolls in a greased 13"x9" baking pan; cover and let rise until double. Bake at 375 degrees for 20 minutes. Drizzle with powdered sugar glaze; serve warm.

A pat of herb butter is heavenly on warm homemade bread. Blend 1/2 cup softened butter and a teaspoon each of chopped fresh parsley, chives and dill. Pack into a crock and chill.

## Louise's Minestrone
## Winter Comfort Soup

*Louise Soweski*
*Woodbridge, NJ*

*I created this recipe one winter during a snowstorm. I wanted a bowl of soup to warm me up! So I started with chicken broth, and began to chop the vegetables I had on hand. Added garlic and ginger for bite. Before I knew it, I had created my own minestrone soup!*

32-oz. container chicken or
    vegetable broth
28-oz. can can whole peeled
    plum tomatoes
1 large carrot, peeled and
    chopped
2 stalks celery, chopped
1 large onion, chopped
3 new potatoes, chopped
2 cloves garlic, minced

1/2-inch piece fresh ginger,
    peeled and diced
1/4 t. Italian seasoning
1/8 t. celery salt
1/8 t. pepper
2 bay leaves
15-1/2 oz. can favorite beans
1 c. frozen peas
1 c. cooked alphabet pasta
2 T. fresh parsley, chopped

Add chicken or vegetable broth to a Dutch oven over medium heat. Add tomatoes with juice, breaking up tomatoes by hand and removing the cores. Add vegetables, garlic, ginger and seasonings. Simmer for 15 to 20 minutes, until vegetables are almost tender; stir in beans and frozen peas. Discard bay leaves; season with additional salt and pepper, if desired. To serve, add cooked pasta to individual soup bowls; ladle soup into bowls. Garnish with parsley and serve. Makes 6 servings.

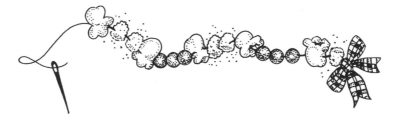

Need something for the kids to do on a snow day? Stringing popcorn is old-fashioned fun. All you need is a big bowl of plain popcorn, a needle and strong thread. They'll be proud to see their popcorn string on the Christmas tree.

## White Bean, Sausage & Mushroom Soup

*Mary Garcia*
*Phoenix, AZ*

*A delicious, hearty soup! We enjoy this with crusty country-style bread and fresh fruit.*

4 slices bacon, chopped
1/2 onion, chopped
12-oz. pkg. sliced mushrooms
14-oz. pkg. smoked mild Italian
   pork sausage link
32-oz. pkg. chicken broth

2  15-1/2 oz. cans cannellini
   beans, drained
1 c. whole milk
salt and pepper to taste
Garnish: chopped fresh basil

Cook bacon in a Dutch oven over medium heat until crisp. Set aside bacon on paper towels; reserve drippings in pan. Add onion and mushrooms to drippings; sauté until golden. Remove with a slotted spoon and set aside. Add sausage to pan; cook until browned and drain. Let cool; slice sausage and set aside. Wipe pan clean with a paper towel; add mushroom mixture, chicken broth and one can beans. Bring to a boil. Stir in milk; process to desired consistency with an immersion blender. Return bacon and sausage to pan; add remaining can of beans. Season with salt and pepper; garnish with basil. Makes 6 to 8 servings.

Soup to go! Tuck a big jar of your best soup, a packet of saltines and a cheery soup bowl into a basket. Sure to be equally appreciated by a friend with the sniffles, or who simply doesn't get enough homemade meals!

# Grandma's Best *Christmas* RECIPES

## Christmas Eve Chicken Alfredo Soup

*Marian Forck*
*Chamois, MO*

*For our family's Christmas Eve dinner after church, I wanted to come up with a recipe that my late husband Bernie could eat. He was on dialysis and could no longer have tomatoes or potatoes. So, this is what I came up with. I served with Cheddar biscuits...everyone enjoyed the Christmas Eve meal!*

4 to 5 boneless, skinless
    chicken breasts
2 chicken bouillon cubes
1 c. cooked broccoli, chopped
1/2 c. carrots, peeled and
    chopped
1/2 c. onion, chopped
1/2 c. red, orange, yellow
    and/or green peppers, diced

2 T. plus 1/2 t. garlic, minced
2 15-oz. jars Alfredo sauce
2 t. Italian seasoning
pepper to taste
12-oz. pkg. fettuccine pasta,
    uncooked
Garnish: grated Parmesan
    cheese

In a large saucepan over medium heat, cover chicken breasts with water. Simmer until chicken is tender, 20 to 30 minutes. Set aside chicken to cool, reserving 2 cups broth in pan. Add bouillon cubes to reserved broth. Add broccoli, carrots, onion, peppers and garlic to broth; bring to a boil. Cover and simmer over medium heat for 5 minutes, or until vegetables are tender. Cube chicken; add to broth along with Alfredo sauce, Italian seasoning and pepper. Simmer for 5 more minutes. Separately cook pasta according to package directions; drain and add to soup. Simmer until heated through. Serve Parmesan cheese on the side, so guests can add their own. Makes 8 servings.

For the most flavorful chicken soup, use bone-in, skin-on chicken. Skin and bones are easily removed after the chicken is cooked. Chill the soup overnight...skim off any fat before rewarming and serving your delicious soup.

# Snowy-Day Soups & Breads

## Quick Sunday Bread

*Suzanne Varnes*
*Toccoa, GA*

*This is my favorite bread recipe that my mom would make often.*
*So good served warm, with a bit of butter spread on top.*

1 env. active dry yeast
1/4 c. very warm water, about
　　110 to 115 degrees
1 c. cool water
2 T. sugar

2 T. butter, melted
1 t. salt
3 c. all-purpose flour
Garnish: softened butter

In a large bowl, dissolve yeast in warm water; let stand for 5 minutes.
Add remaining ingredients except garnish; mix well. Pour batter into a
well-greased 9"x5" loaf pan. Cover and let rise for one hour. Uncover;
bake at 450 degrees for 15 minutes. Turn oven to 300 degrees; bake for
30 additional minutes. Brush bread with additional butter while still
warm. Turn out of pan to cool; slice and serve. Makes one loaf.

For a thoughtful gift, purchase a calendar and fill in birthdays,
anniversaries and other important family events...a nice gift
for those new to the family!

# Grandma's Best *Christmas* RECIPES

## Stuffed Pepper Soup

*Charlotte Smith*
*Huntingdon, PA*

*Easy to make...yummy to eat! This recipe was given to me by a former co-worker. We used to have a soup sale and this soup was always the first to sell out.*

2 lbs. ground beef
8 c. water
28-oz. can diced tomatoes
28-oz. can tomato juice
2 c. green peppers, chopped

1/4 c. sugar
2 c. instant rice, uncooked
2 cubes beef bouillon
2 t. salt
1 t. pepper

Brown beef in a large soup pot over medium heat; drain. Add water, undrained tomatoes and remaining ingredients; bring to a boil. Reduce heat to medium-low. Cover and simmer for 30 to 40 minutes, until green peppers are tender. Makes 10 to 15 servings.

## Split Pea Soup

*Paula Marchesi*
*Auburn, PA*

*When you have a busy schedule, the slow cooker is the answer. Quick & easy...anyone can do it! I've made this soup for many years and it's a sure thing in our household.*

2 c. dried split peas, rinsed
  and sorted
8 c. water
2 onions, chopped

2 carrots, peeled and sliced
6 cubes chicken bouillon
1 t. salt
1/4 t. pepper

Combine all ingredients in a 4-quart slow cooker; stir. Cover and cook on low setting for 8 to 9 hours. Makes 8 servings.

Be prepared for a winter snowstorm! Stock your pantry with canned vegetables, creamy soups, rice mixes, pasta and other handy meal-makers.

# Snowy-Day Soups & Breads

## Creamy Potato-Leek Soup

*Carolyn Deckard*
*Bedford, IN*

*I found this great recipe for a meatless soup in one of Mom's church recipe books a few years ago. I have made it several times... it's perfect for chilly evenings.*

1/4 c. butter
4 c. leeks, cut into 1/2-inch slices
1/4 c. carrots, peeled and finely
   chopped
5 c. russet potatoes, peeled
   and cubed

4 c. water
4 t. chicken bouillon granules
15-oz. jar Alfredo pasta sauce
salt and pepper to taste
2 T. fresh chives, chopped

Melt butter in a large saucepan over medium-high heat; add leeks and carrots. Cook for 15 minutes, stirring occasionally. Add potatoes, water and chicken bouillon; bring to a boil. Reduce heat to medium. Cover and simmer for 25 to 35 minutes, stirring occasionally. Stir in pasta sauce; simmer for another 5 to 6 minutes, until heated through. Season with salt and pepper as desired. Remove from heat and stir in chives. Makes 8 servings.

I truly believe that if we keep telling the Christmas story, singing the Christmas songs and living the Christmas spirit, we can bring joy and happiness and peace to this world.
– Norman Vincent Peale

# Grandma's Best *Christmas* RECIPES

## Our Favorite Chili

*Angela Beecher*
*Ponchatoula, LA*

*This recipe was shared with me by a family friend. I made some changes along the way, and now it is my favorite chili to make when the weather turns cooler. It's tasty with cornbread, too. I like to use one can of original flavor tomatoes with chiles and one can of mild.*

2 lbs. ground beef
1/2 c. onion, diced
29-oz. can tomato sauce
2 10-oz. cans diced tomatoes
   with green chiles
2 15-1/2 oz. cans pinto beans,
   lightly drained

2 c. water
2 to 3 t. chili powder
2 t. ground cumin
2 t. salt
1-1/2 t. pepper
Optional: shredded Cheddar
   cheese

Brown beef in a soup pot over medium heat; drain. Add onion and cook for one minute, or until beginning to soften. Add tomato sauce, undrained tomatoes and remaining ingredients; stir well and bring to a simmer. Simmer for about one hour. Garnish with cheese, if desired. Makes 8 to 10 servings.

For old-fashioned charm, group together an assortment of vintage tin graters on a tabletop or mantel, tuck a tea light under each and enjoy their cozy flickering lights.

# Snowy-Day Soups & Breads

## Sweet Potato Chili

*Debra Johnson*
*Myrtle Beach, SC*

*At my house, we all love chili! This sweet potato chili is a yummy variation from our usual. If I have roast turkey left from the holidays, I'll use it in place of the chicken. Garnish with a dollop of sour cream and some crushed white tortilla chips.*

2 T. oil
2 c. sweet potatoes, peeled and
    cut into 1/2-inch chunks
1 c. onion, chopped
1 c. red pepper, chopped
1 to 2 c. chicken broth

14-1/2 oz. can petite diced
    tomatoes
1-1/4 oz. pkg. chili
    seasoning mix
2 c. cooked chicken, diced

Heat oil in a large skillet over medium-high heat. Add sweet potatoes, onion and red pepper; cook and stir for 5 minutes, or until lightly golden. Stir in tomatoes with juice, chicken broth and chili seasoning; bring to a boil. Reduce heat to medium-low; stir in chicken. Cover and simmer for 15 minutes, stirring occasionally, or until sweet potatoes are tender. Makes 6 servings.

Bake up some sweet and tangy cranberry corn muffins to serve with your favorite chili. Just stir dried cranberries and a little orange zest into a cornbread muffin mix. Bake as directed on the package...serve topped with a pat of butter.

# Grandma's Best Christmas RECIPES

## Grandma Olney's Soup

*Joan Olney
Marathon, IA*

*This soup was originally from the kitchen of John Adams (yes, the president) who was a distant cousin of my great-grandmother's. She had eight children and this soup could keep them fed cheaply. Great-Grandmother would make a pot and put it on the back of the stove, and it would be there all day. It's that easy. I know this sounds odd, but it's delicious, especially with thick slices of crusty bread.*

1/2 lb. bacon, diced
2 to 3 potatoes, peeled and diced
3/4 c. onion, diced
6 to 8 c. water

salt and pepper to taste
16-oz. pkg. Amish-style or
    egg noodles, uncooked

Combine all ingredients except noodles in a large soup pot over medium heat. Bring to a boil; add noodles. Simmer for 15 to 20 minutes, until potatoes and noodles are tender. Makes 6 servings.

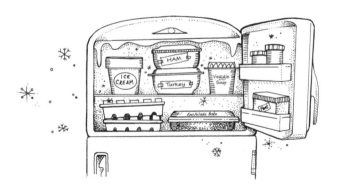

Grandma knew that it's almost as easy to make a big pot of
soup as a small one! Make double batches of family favorites
like chili and freeze half for later. On a busy day, you'll be
so glad to have home-cooked soup to heat up for dinnertime.

# Snowy-Day Soups & Breads

## Savory Soup Crackers

Beckie Apple
Grannis, AR

*These tasty crackers are very versatile! They are really good with a hot bowl of tomato soup...I love them as appetizers, too. I make these around the holidays and put them in pint jars as gifts.*

3 9-oz. pkgs. oyster crackers
3/4 c. oil
3 T. ranch seasoning mix
3 T. red pepper flakes
3 T. Italian seasoning
1 T. garlic powder

Add crackers to a one-gallon plastic zipping bag; set aside. Combine oil and all seasonings in a 2-cup glass measuring cup; whisk to mix well. Pour oil mixture over crackers; close bag securely. Shake and turn bag over to mix seasonings thoroughly into crackers. Lay bag flat on the counter; shake and turn bag every 30 minutes for about 2 hours. Let stand for another 2 hours and serve. Makes 8 to 10 servings.

## Warm-Up Soup

Andrea Czarniecki
Northville, MI

*This is the soup everyone wants when they come in from sledding or skiing! It warms you to your bones and to your toes. Quick & easy to make...yummy and very filling!*

1 lb. ground pork sausage
1 onion, chopped
3 cloves garlic, minced
10 to 12 new redskin potatoes, chopped
4 to 6 c. chicken broth
1 c. milk
1 t. butter
2 to 3 c. fresh kale, chopped
Garnish: grated Parmesan cheese

In a skillet over medium heat, cook sausage with onion and garlic until browned and crumbled; drain and set aside. Meanwhile, combine potatoes and chicken broth in a large saucepan over medium heat. Bring to a boil; boil gently until potatoes are tender. Add sausage mixture; simmer for 25 to 30 minutes. Add milk, butter and kale. Simmer for 5 minutes, or until kale is wilted. Ladle into bowls; top with Parmesan cheese. Serves 6 to 8.

## Great-Grandma's Christmas Fruit Soup

*Kimberly Redeker*
*Savoy, IL*

*This is a sweet soup, more like a dessert or snack, and it's great served warm or cold. It's an old Norwegian recipe called sot suppe. The cinnamon brings a holiday warmth to all the various fruit. It's a good-for-you treat from my great-grandma!*

1-1/2 c. dried apples
1-1/2 c. dried apricots
1-1/2 c. dried peaches
1-1/2 c. golden raisins
1-1/2 c. dark raisins
1-1/2 c. prunes

1/2 c. dried cherries
1/2 c. long-cooking tapioca, uncooked
2 64-oz. bottles apple juice
5 4-inch cinnamon sticks

Chop all of the fruit into small pieces; add to a large stockpot along with remaining ingredients. Bring to a boil over over medium heat; reduce heat to medium-low. Simmer, stirring occasionally, for 30 to 45 minutes, until tapioca is cooked. Discard cinnamon sticks before serving. Makes 15 to 20 servings.

Make memories with little ones by creating a simple paper chain. Use it to decorate the tree, or count down to the big day with each loop!

# Coming Home for Christmas Dinner

# Grandma's Best Christmas RECIPES

## Yorkshire Pudding Casserole

*Sherry Rhoads*
*Grove, OK*

*My grandmother was from England, so when I was a child, Yorkshire pudding was on every holiday table. This is my take on a family tradition. I started making it when my boys were young...they loved it and I still fix it today. My oldest son is now in his forties!*

1 lb. ground beef sirloin
4 eggs, divided
1/4 c. rolled oats, uncooked
1 t. Worcestershire sauce
1/2 t. salt
1/4 t. pepper

1 c. milk
2 T. butter, melted
1 c. all-purpose flour
1 t. baking powder
20-oz. jar beef gravy, heated

In a large bowl, combine beef, one beaten egg, oats, Worcestershire sauce, salt and pepper. Mix well; form into 16 meatballs. Arrange meatballs in an 8"x8" baking pan sprayed with non-stick spray; set aside. In a bowl, beat remaining eggs until frothy. Add milk and melted butter; blend well and set aside. In a separate bowl, combine flour and baking powder; mix well and add to egg mixture. Stir only until blended together; pour batter over meatballs. Bake, uncovered, at 350 degrees for 50 minutes, or until batter is puffed and golden. Serve with hot gravy. Makes 6 servings.

Mix & match...set a festive table with items you already have! Green transferware serving bowls, sparkling white porcelain dinner plates and ruby-red stemmed glasses combine beautifully with Christmas dinnerware and with each other.

# Coming Home for Christmas Dinner

## Nonna's Mac & Cheese

*Linda Kilgore*
*Kittanning, PA*

*I have been making this macaroni & cheese for years. My kids loved it, and now my grandkids love it too. I make it for holidays and special occasions. Everywhere I take it, there is never enough!*

16-oz. pkg. large pasta shells, uncooked
1/2 c. butter, sliced
salt and pepper to taste
1 c. soft bread crumbs

7-oz. pkg. sliced Gouda cheese
8-oz. pkg. pasteurized process cheese, cubed
2 c. milk
1/2 c. panko bread crumbs

Cook pasta according to package directions; drain. Transfer pasta to a buttered 13"x9" baking pan. Add butter and stir until melted; season with salt and pepper. Stir in soft bread crumbs. Layer Gouda cheese slices on top; add processed cheese cubes. Pour milk over all. Cover with aluminum foil and bake at 425 degrees for 30 minutes. Uncover and stir well; return to oven and bake another 15 minutes, or until bubbly. Sprinkle with panko bread crumbs; bake another 10 minutes, or until golden. Serves 10.

Be sure to ask your kids about their favorite holiday foods as you plan for the season's occasions. You may find you have "traditions" in your family that you weren't even aware of!

## Squisito Lasagna

*Kimberly Oswald*
*Conway, SC*

*Delicious! This is my go-to recipe whenever I need to bring a dish somewhere...everyone who has ever tasted it, loves it. I received this recipe from my mother-in-law in the late 1970s. I didn't know how to cook, and she told me if I could layer a baking pan, I could make this, because all the flavors are in the cheeses and the marinara sauce. This also tastes great on the second night. Sometimes I make it the night before I bake it, so all the flavors can infuse.*

12 lasagna noodles, uncooked
1 lb. ground beef
2 t. garlic salt, or to taste
1/4 c. grated Parmesan cheese, or to taste
2 to 3 t. olive oil
24-oz. jar marinara sauce, divided

1 lb. smoked Gouda cheese, shredded and divided
1 lb. plain or Italian herb provolone cheese, shredded and divided

Cook noodles according to package directions; drain and cool. Meanwhile, brown beef in a skillet over medium heat. Drain; season with garlic salt and Parmesan cheese. Coat the bottom and sides of a 13"x9" baking pan with olive oil. Spread 1/3 of marinara sauce in bottom of pan. Arrange 4 lasagna noodles over sauce, overlapping slightly. Layer with 1/2 of beef mixture and 1/2 of each cheese, reserving a small amount of each cheese for topping. Layer with another 4 noodles, another 1/3 of pasta sauce and remaining beef and cheeses. Layer remaining 4 noodles on top; spread remaining sauce over noodles. Bake, uncovered, at 350 degrees for 20 minutes, or until hot and bubbly. Sprinkle with reserved cheeses. Return to oven for 3 minutes, or until cheese melts. Cut into squares to serve. Makes 10 to 12 servings.

Warm garlic bread is a must with pasta! Blend 1/2 cup softened butter and 2 teaspoons minced garlic; spread over a split loaf of Italian bread. Bake at 350 degrees for 8 minutes, or until hot, then broil briefly, until golden. Slice and serve.

# Coming Home for Christmas Dinner

## Linguine with Prosciutto & Green Olives

*Mia Rossi*
*Charlotte, NC*

*This pasta dish reminds of my Italian grandmother's cooking. We enjoy it either as a simple meal with a crisp salad, or as a side with roasted or skillet-braised meats.*

9-oz. pkg. refrigerated linguine
   pasta, uncooked
1/4 c. olive oil
2 oz. thinly sliced deli prosciutto,
   cut into 1/4-inch wide strips

1/2 c. green onions, thinly sliced
3-oz. jar green olives with
   pimentos, drained
1 c. cherry tomatoes, halved
2/3 c. grated Parmesan cheese

Cook pasta according to package directions; drain. Transfer to a serving bowl; cover and set aside. Meanwhile, heat oil in a skillet over medium-high heat. Add prosciutto and cook for 3 to 4 minutes, stirring often, until lightly golden. Add onions; cook and stir just until beginning to soften. Stir in olives and tomatoes; cook for 2 minutes, or until heated through. To serve, spoon prosciutto mixture over pasta; toss lightly. Garnish with Parmesan cheese and serve. Makes 4 servings.

For a simple yet pretty centerpiece, set 2 or 3 pillar candles on a platter. Tuck vintage Christmas ornaments around the base to add sparkle.

# Grandma's Best Christmas RECIPES

## Mimi's Western Meatloaf

*Glenda Ballard*
*West Columbia, SC*

*This recipe came from my Aunt Mimi, my mother's sister. As the young bride of a military man in 1967, Mimi left sunny South Carolina and a large family for the first time, for their duty station in snowy Omaha, Nebraska! On their arrival, her next-door neighbor welcomed them with this delicious meatloaf. It was a kindness my aunt never forgot. She immediately sent this recipe home to us, and it's been a family favorite ever since.*

1-1/2 lbs. ground beef
2 T. onion, chopped
1-1/2 c. soft bread crumbs
1-1/2 t. salt
1/4 t. pepper

1-3/4 c. milk
1/2 c. all-purpose flour
3 to 4 potatoes, peeled and
  quartered
10-3/4 oz. can tomato soup

In a large bowl, lightly mix beef, onion, bread crumbs and seasonings. Add milk and flour a little at a time. Shape into one or 2 loaves. Place in a buttered 13"x9" baking pan, setting 2 loaves side-by-side. Arrange potatoes around loaf; spoon soup over meatloaf and potatoes. Cover and bake at 350 degrees for one hour, checking after 40 minutes. Serves 6.

## Easy Beef & Noodles

*Pamela Layman*
*La Porte, IN*

*Winters in northwest Indiana can be brutal, but with a plate of this delicious dish our family was instantly warmed up!*

3 lbs. stew beef cubes
2 4-oz. cans sliced mushrooms,
  drained
2 10-3/4 oz. cans golden
  mushroom soup

1.35-oz. pkg. onion soup mix
1 c. Chianti wine or beef broth
cooked noodles or rice

Combine beef cubes and mushrooms in a lightly greased 13"x9" baking pan; set aside. In a bowl, blend mushroom soup, soup mix and wine or broth; spoon over beef mixture. Cover with aluminum foil. Bake at 325 degrees for 3-1/2 to 4 hours. To serve, spoon over cooked noodles or rice. Makes 6 servings.

# Coming Home for Christmas Dinner

## Angel Hair with Meat Sauce

*Jo Ann*
*Gooseberry Patch*

*We love the aroma of this homemade sauce simmering on
a Sunday afternoon. Serve with grated Parmesan cheese...
and pass the garlic bread, please!*

2 T. oil
1/4 c. onion, chopped
1/4 c. celery, chopped
1 clove garlic, minced
1/2 lb. ground lean beef
1/2 lb. ground lean pork
2 6-oz. cans tomato paste
2 c. tomatoes, diced

1 c. sliced mushrooms
1/2 c. green pepper, chopped
2 T. grated Parmesan cheese
2 T. fresh parsley, minced
1 t. fresh oregano, snipped
1-1/2 t. salt
16-oz. pkg. angel hair pasta,
    uncooked

Heat oil in a skillet over medium heat. Add onion, celery and garlic;
sauté for 2 minutes. Add beef and pork; cook until browned and drain.
Add remaining ingredients except pasta. Cover and simmer over
medium-low heat for 1-1/4 to 1-1/2 hours, stirring often. Shortly
before serving time, cook pasta according to package directions; drain.
Serve meat sauce ladled over pasta. Serves 8.

Fill a glass trifle bowl with shiny glass balls and add sparkly
strands of beads around the bowl's edges...an easy
centerpiece to put together in a jiffy!

## Grandma's Southern-Style Chicken & Dumplin's

*Julie Hutson*
*Callahan, FL*

*One of my fondest memories of my grandma is sitting in her kitchen, watching her roll out dumplings. She never measured out anything, and it always turned out mouthwatering perfect! On rare occasions, I will make my own dumplings, but I have found that the frozen dumplings taste authentic and save so much time.*

3-1/2 lb. chicken, cut up
salt and pepper to taste
12-oz. pkg. frozen homestyle
    dumplings, uncooked

2 T. all-purpose flour
1/2 c. milk
1/4 c. butter

In a large stockpot, cover chicken pieces with water; season with salt and pepper. Bring to a boil over high heat; reduce heat to medium-low. Cover and simmer for 2 hours, stirring occasionally, or until chicken easily falls off the bone. Remove chicken to cool, reserving broth in stockpot. Shred chicken, discarding bones and skin. Add more water to existing broth to fill stockpot 1/2 full. Bring to a boil once again. One by one, drop each frozen dumpling into the boiling water. Once all are added, stir well; reduce heat to medium. Return shredded chicken to stockpot. Simmer for 30 minutes, stirring often. In a small bowl, whisk together flour and milk, making a thin paste. Slowly pour flour mixture into stockpot. Continue to cook and stir until thick and bubbly. Add butter; stir to melt. Remove from heat; let stand for 15 minutes to cool and thicken a little more, then serve. Serves 8.

The secret of the best Christmases is everybody
doing the same things all at the same time.
–Robert P. Tristram Coffin

# Coming Home for Christmas Dinner

## Chicken & Sausage Cacciatore
*Shirley Howie*
*Foxboro, MA*

*I like to put my trusty slow cooker to work during the busy holiday season. This dish is perfect for those cold winter evenings, hearty and full of comfort and joy!*

1 lb. Italian pork sausage, sliced
   1/2-inch thick
1 lb. boneless, skinless chicken
   breasts, cut into 1-inch cubes
2 T. oil
1 green pepper, cut into
   1/2-inch strips
1 c. sliced mushrooms

1 onion, sliced and separated
   into rings
1/2 t. dried oregano
1/2 t. dried basil
1-1/2 c. Italian-style tomato
   sauce
cooked pasta or rice
Garnish: grated Parmesan cheese

In a large skillet over medium heat, lightly brown sausage and chicken pieces in oil; drain. Layer vegetables in a 5-quart slow cooker; top with sausage mixture. Sprinkle with herbs; top with tomato sauce. Cover and cook on low setting for 3 to 4 hours. Uncover during the last 30 minutes of cooking time to allow the sauce to thicken. Serve over cooked pasta or rice, topped with grated Parmesan cheese. Makes 4 to 6 servings.

Slow-cooker recipes are perfect for family meals after a day of Christmas shopping. For an easy side, whip up a marinated salad to keep in the fridge...cut up crunchy veggies and toss with zesty Italian salad dressing.

# Grandma's Best Christmas RECIPES

## Must-Have Holiday Meat Pie

*Lisa Hains*
*Ontario, Canada*

*Here is my most-loved holiday recipe. This pie is wonderful enjoyed with appetizers and a salad, or as a highlight to your traditional holiday feast...yum! When I was a young wife and mother, my husband and I lived in a northern Canadian city, where he ministered for a church. There we met many wonderful warm-hearted people. Most of the locals were of the French-Canadian culture. Their "tourtiere," or French-Canadian meat pie, was a holiday tradition, generously shared when visitors dropped in. Over the years, my husband and I developed our very own favorite version that is an absolute must-have at our family parties. We might be in serious trouble if these pies didn't appear at the holiday, hot from the oven.*

1 lb. ground beef, pork, veal
   or a combination
1 onion, chopped
1 carrot, peeled and grated
2-1/2 T. all-purpose flour
10-3/4 oz. can cream of chicken
   or mushroom soup
2 c. frozen diced hashbrown
   potatoes
1 to 1-1/2 c. water

1/2 t. garlic powder
1/2 t. dried sage
1/4 t. dried thyme
1/4 t. poultry seasoning
1/2 t. pepper
salt to taste
2 9-inch deep-dish pie crusts
Optional: small amount cream
   or milk

Cook meat in a Dutch oven over medium heat until browned and caramelized. Add onion and carrot; continue cooking until meat is richly browned. Sprinkle with flour; mix thoroughly. Stir in soup, frozen hashbrowns and enough water to create a creamy consistency. (Mixture will thicken as it bakes.) Stir in seasonings. Spoon filling into one pie crust. Top with remaining crust; seal and pinch or crimp edges. Cut several vent slits in crust. If desired, brush crust with a little cream or milk. Set pie on a baking sheet. Bake at 350 degrees for 60 minutes, or until bottom crust is completely baked. If top crust begins to overbrown in the last 20 to 25 minutes, cover loosely with a piece of aluminum foil. Cool for several minutes; cut into wedges. Serves 6 to 8.

# *Coming Home for Christmas Dinner*

## Cheddar Beef Pie

*Georgia Muth*
*Penn Valley, CA*

*My grandma used her pie plates daily. Along with all the scrumptious fruit pies she made, a good meal was often served pie-style. This is one of my favorites.*

1 lb. ground beef
1 egg, beaten
1/3 c. onion, diced
1 c. corn flake cereal, crushed
    and divided
2 T. barbecue sauce
1 t. salt

1/8 t. pepper
1/2 c. celery, diced
Optional: 1/2 c. sliced
    mushrooms
2 T. butter, divided
1-1/2 c. shredded sharp Cheddar
    cheese

In a large bowl, combine beef, egg, onion, 3/4 cup crushed corn flakes, barbecue sauce and seasonings. Mix well; press mixture into the bottom and sides of an ungreased 9" pie plate. Bake, uncovered, at 400 degrees for 15 minutes. Remove from oven; carefully drain drippings from pan. Reduce oven to 350 degrees. In a skillet over medium heat, sauté celery and mushrooms, if using, in one tablespoon butter. Add cheese; toss lightly and spoon into hot beef crust. Melt remaining butter with remaining cereal crumbs; sprinkle over cheese mixture. Bake, uncovered, at 350 degrees for 12 minutes. Cut into wedges and serve. Makes 6 servings.

Sweet vintage pie plates can easily be found at tag sales and flea markets...maybe even in Mom's cupboard! Words stamped inside like "Flaky Crust" or "Mellow Rich Pie" make them so charming. They're just right for sharing a pie with a special friend.

# Grandma's Best Christmas RECIPES

## Grandma Barr's Ham Loaf

*Becky Myers*
*Ashland, OH*

*My grandmother always made this ham loaf for every family gathering. It is a real comfort food and also makes great sandwiches the next day, if you have any left. I halve this recipe, since we don't have a big family, and it always turns out well. I get the meats pre-ground at our local meat market.*

1-1/2 lbs. ground ham
1-1/2 lbs. ground pork
1 c. saltine crackers, crushed

2 eggs, beaten
1/4 c. milk

In a large bowl, combine all ingredients; mix with your hands and shape into a loaf. Place in an ungreased 13"x9" baking pan. May also make 2 smaller loaves and freeze one for later after baking. Bake, uncovered, at 350 degrees for one hour. During the last 10 minutes, pour Glaze over loaf. Remove loaf to a platter; pour glaze from pan over loaf. Slice and serve. Serves 8.

### Glaze:

1 c. brown sugar, packed
1/4 c. water
1 T. vinegar

1 T. dry mustard
1 t. ground cloves

Combine all ingredients in a 2-cup glass measuring cup; mix well.

Baked sweet potatoes are delicious with baked ham. Pierce potatoes several times with a fork and put them right on the oven rack. At 325 degrees, they'll be tender in about one hour. Top with butter and sprinkle with cinnamon-sugar. It couldn't be easier!

# Coming Home for Christmas Dinner

## Cranberry-Glazed Baked Ham

*Pattie Prescott*
*Manchester, NH*

*This is a treasured recipe that we look forward to every Christmas.
I have fond memories of Christmas dinners at Grandma's house and
now love making this for my family every year. The currant jelly can
sometimes be hard to find closer to Christmas, so try to plan ahead
and look for it several weeks ahead.*

5 to 6-lb. fully cooked
    bone-in ham
12-oz. pkg. fresh cranberries
15-oz. can whole-berry
    cranberry sauce

12-oz. jar currant jelly
1 c. light corn syrup
1/2 t. ground ginger

Bake ham according to package directions, or as preferred. Meanwhile,
combine remaining ingredients in a saucepan. Simmer over medium
heat for 10 to 15 minutes, until cranberries burst, stirring occasionally.
If desired, brush warm glaze over ham 2 times during the last 30 minutes
of baking. Slice ham; serve with warm glaze as a sauce on the side.
Serves 12.

Traveling for the holidays? Have little ones leave Santa
a note with instructions telling him where you'll be
visiting the night before Christmas!

113

# Grandma's Best *Christmas* RECIPES

## Chicken Piccata with Artichokes
*Regina Vining*
*Warwick, RI*

*This was Gram's favorite dish for special occasions. She served it over angel hair pasta, garnished with thin slices of lemon. So good...I'm glad she passed this along to me!*

4 boneless, skinless chicken
    breasts, cut in half
3/4 c. all-purpose flour
1/2 t. Italian seasoning
1/8 t. garlic powder
1/4 t. salt
1/8 t. pepper
2 T. olive oil
1 onion, diced

1 clove garlic, minced
1/2 c. white wine or water
14-1/2 oz. can chicken broth
14-oz. can artichokes, drained
    and chopped, liquid reserved
2 T. lemon juice
2 T. butter
1/4 c. jarred capers with liquid

Flatten chicken breasts to 1/2-inch thick; set aside. Combine flour and seasonings on a plate; coat chicken lightly in mixture. Heat olive oil in a large skillet over medium-high heat. Add chicken and cook for 2 minutes per side, or until golden. Remove chicken to a plate, reserving drippings in skillet. Add onion and garlic to skillet; cook and stir until translucent, about 5 minutes. Add wine or water to skillet. Increase heat to high and simmer for 4 to 5 minutes, until liquid is reduced by half. Add chicken broth, artichokes with reserved liquid and lemon juice to skillet; stir. Return chicken to skillet. Reduce heat to medium and simmer for about 20 minutes, until sauce is thickened. Just before serving, stir in butter and capers with liquid. Serves 4 to 6.

Start a sweet new tradition at dinner.
Hand out paper star cut-outs and have
each person write down what they're
happiest for since last Christmas.

# Coming Home for Christmas Dinner

## Glazed Apricot Chicken

*Sandy Coffey*
*Cincinnati, OH*

*A great-tasting special chicken recipe to share anytime throughout the Christmas season. Serve with steamed rice and a green vegetable.*

4 boneless, skinless chicken
   breasts
2 T. butter
1/4 to 1/2 c. chopped pecans

salt and pepper to taste
1/2 c. apricot preserves
1 T. white vinegar
1/4 t. ground ginger

Pat chicken breasts dry with paper towels; set aside. Melt butter in a skillet over medium heat. Add chicken and pecans; cook for 8 to 10 minutes, turning occasionally, until golden and chicken juices run clear when pierced. Transfer chicken to a serving dish, reserving juices in skillet. Season chicken lightly with salt and pepper; cover to keep warm. For the glaze, stir remaining ingredients into reserved juices in skillet. Cook and stir over medium heat for 2 minutes, or until heated through. Spoon glaze over chicken and serve. Makes 4 servings.

Bundle up the kids and take a ride to see the holiday lights around town. Bring cozy blankets and plump pillows... the kids can even wear their jammies! You'll be making memories together that will last for many years.

# Grandma's Best *Christmas* RECIPES

## Chicken, Shrimp & Bowties

*Beverley MacNeil*
*Ontario, Canada*

*I have been making this dish on Christmas Eve for several years now. I used to ask my family what we were going to have for supper on Christmas Eve, but stopped asking because it was always the same answer. "Our traditional dish, Mom. That's all we want!" Now my boys are grown and have their own families, but this is still our Christmas Eve dish. Last year, I suggested we have something different, and everyone objected! So, it's still our tradition. I like to serve warm Cheddar biscuits with this.*

2 16-oz. pkgs. bowtie pasta,
    uncooked
3 to 4 boneless, skinless chicken
    breasts, cut into bite-size
    pieces

1 to 2 T. oil
2 lbs. uncooked shrimp, peeled
    and cleaned
2 1.3-oz. pkgs. Parma Rosa
    sauce mix

Cook pasta according to package directions; drain and return to pan. Meanwhile, in a large skillet over medium heat, cook chicken in a small amount of oil, turning occasionally, until chicken juices run clear when pierced. Remove chicken from pan; set aside. Add a bit more oil to skillet if necessary. Add shrimp and cook for 5 to 10 minutes, until pink. In a small saucepan, prepare sauce mix according to package directions. Add chicken and shrimp to cooked pasta; mix well. Spoon sauce over all and stir to coat well. Serves 6 to 8.

Serve a cozy holiday dinner...pull your table and chairs right up next to the fireplace. Keep decorations simple and open a gift or 2 after dinner as an extra treat.

# *Coming Home for Christmas Dinner*

## Dan's Old-Fashioned Italian Mac & Cheese

*Dan Scungio*
*Williamsburg, VA*

*My mother always made tomato macaroni & cheese just for me, since the rest of the family wouldn't eat it. It brings back special memories for me as a child growing through the years. This is how my mother made it and I didn't change a thing, other than adding Italian seasoning. I hope you enjoy it as well.*

16-oz. pkg. medium pasta
    shells, uncooked
1/4 c. butter
1/4 c. all-purpose flour
3 c. milk
1 T. Italian seasoning
1/2 t. garlic powder
1/2 t. salt

1/4 to 1/2 t. pepper
2 8-oz. pkgs. extra-sharp
    Cheddar cheese, shredded
    or diced
14-1/2 oz. can diced tomatoes
1/4 c. Italian-seasoned dry bread
    crumbs

Cook pasta shells according to package directions, one minute less than directed; drain and return to pan. Meanwhile, melt butter in a large Dutch oven over medium heat. Add flour; cook and stir until bubbly and golden, about 2 minutes. Slowly add milk; cook over medium heat until thickened, whisking often. Stir in seasonings until well combined. Add cheese; whisk until melted and smooth. Add tomatoes with juice; stir well and heat through. Reduce heat to low. Add cheese sauce to cooked pasta, stirring to combine well. Transfer mixture to a greased 3-quart casserole dish. Sprinkle with bread crumbs, just enough to cover the top. Bake, uncovered, at 350 degrees for 35 to 45 minutes, until bubbly and lightly golden. Let stand for a few minutes for sauce to thicken. Serves 9 to 12.

Family photos make terrific gift tags. Just copy, cut out and tie on. No need to write "To" on each tag...everyone can open the packages with their picture!

# Grandma's Best Christmas RECIPES

## Grandma Franceshi's Homemade Ravioli

*Ronica Fronzaglio*
*Monongahela, PA*

*My family would get together every year to make these delicious ravioli. Mom told me that when she was a child, my Grandma Flo would get up early on Christmas morning to make the ravioli!*

1-1/2 lbs. ground beef
1-1/2 lbs. ground pork and
  veal mix
1/4 c. onion, finely chopped
1/4 c. fresh parsley, chopped
2 cloves garlic, minced
1/2 t. celery seed
4 eggs, beaten

8-oz. container grated Romano
  cheese
2 10-oz. pkgs. frozen chopped
  spinach, thawed
salt and pepper to taste
small amount milk
Garnish: favorite red Italian
  pasta sauce

In a large skillet over medium heat, brown meats with onion, parsley, garlic and celery seed; drain and remove from heat. Add eggs and cheese; squeeze out all the water from spinach and add. Mix well. Season with salt and pepper; set aside. To make ravioli, divide Dough into 2 halves. On a floured surface, roll out each half 1/4-inch thick. Cut dough into 2-1/2 inch squares using a ravioli mold or a sharp knife. For each ravioli, top a dough square with one tablespoon meat filling. Top with another square; seal all edges with a fork dipped into milk. To serve, drop ravioli into a stockpot of boiling water; boil for about 7 to 9 minutes. Drain; serve ravioli topped with desired sauce. Makes 12 servings.

## Dough:

4 c. all-purpose flour
6 to 10 egg yolks, beaten

1 c. milk, warmed
1 t. salt

Combine all ingredients; mix with your hands until dough forms.

# Coming Home for Christmas Dinner

## Pierogi Pasta Shells

*Kimberly Wallace*
*Dennison, OH*

*We love pierogies! So I thought, why not create my own version. I took these to a Christmas party...they won rave reviews! I also took home an empty pan, with not a crumb to be found. Talk about a comfort food...these are so good!*

26 jumbo pasta shells, divided
   and uncooked
32-oz. pkg. mashed potatoes,
   warmed
1 T. dried, minced onions
1/2 t. garlic salt

1/2 t. onion salt
8-oz. pkg. shredded Cheddar
   cheese, divided
2 to 3 T. green onions, sliced
1.1-oz. pkg. potato topping
1 t. butter, diced

Cook pasta shells according to package directions; drain well. (Reserve remaining shells for another recipe.) Meanwhile, heat potatoes according to package directions; transfer to a large bowl. Add dried onions, salts and one cup cheese; mix well. Using a small spoon or a melon ball scoop, fill cooked shells with potato mixture. Arrange stuffed shells in a greased 13"x9" baking pan. Top with remaining cheese, green onions and potato topping; dot with butter. Bake, uncovered, at 350 degrees for 30 to 45 minutes, until heated through and cheese is melted. Makes 8 servings.

The more the merrier! Why not invite a neighbor or a college student who might be spending the holiday alone to share in the Christmas feast?

# Grandma's Best Christmas RECIPES

## Grandma's Swedish Meatballs
*Summer Orbin*
*Pleasant Hope, MO*

*I can remember how yummy this smelled when I walked into my grandma's house. It still does! My family doesn't love onions, so I often use onion powder instead. I usually serve with mashed potatoes, buttered corn and hot rolls. These meatballs freeze well and make a great meatball sub.*

2 lbs. ground beef
1/2 c. rolled oats, uncooked
1 egg, beaten
1 c. milk
1/4 c. onion, minced
1 T. sugar
1 T. Worcestershire sauce
1/4 t. dry mustard
2 t. salt
1/4 t. pepper
1-1/2 c. all-purpose flour

In a large bowl, combine all ingredients except flour. Mix well; scoop into large meatballs. Roll in flour; arrange in an ungreased 13"x9" baking pan. Bake, uncovered, at 350 degrees for 20 to 50 minutes, until browned and cooked through. Spoon Sauce over meatballs. Bake, uncovered, at 325 degrees for one hour. Meatballs may also be browned in a skillet; drain and simmer in sauce. Makes 6 to 8 servings.

## Sauce:

1 c. tomato sauce or juice
1/2 c. water
5 T. vinegar
1/2 c. brown sugar, packed
1/2 c. onion, chopped
1/2 c. catsup
1-1/4 oz. pkg. spaghetti
   sauce mix
2 t. Worcestershire sauce
1/2 t. chili powder
1/4 t. dry mustard
1/4 t. pepper

Mix together all ingredients in a saucepan. Simmer over low heat for 5 minutes, stirring often.

# *Coming Home for Christmas Dinner*

## Garlic Herb Butter Roast Beef
*Paula Marchesi*
*Auburn, PA*

*I've always enjoyed the holidays, even Christmas in July!*
*I've been making this for years, and it's delicious. If there's*
*any leftovers, it makes a great sandwich.*

5 to 5-1/2 lb. beef top
   sirloin roast
1 c. butter, softened
2 shallots, minced
4 cloves garlic, minced
1 T. fresh parsley, chopped
1 t. fresh thyme, chopped

1 t. fresh rosemary, chopped
1 t. fresh oregano, chopped
salt and pepper to taste
2 red onions, quartered
1 head garlic, halved
Optional: fresh rosemary and
   oregano sprigs

Let roast stand at room temperature at least 30 minutes before cooking. In a bowl, stir together butter, shallots, minced garlic and all seasonings. Rub half of butter mixture all over roast until evenly coated. Place roast in a large Dutch oven, fat-side up; arrange onions and garlic around roast. Bake, uncovered, at 400 degrees for 25 to 30 minutes, until golden. Decrease oven temperature to 350 degrees; spoon remaining butter mixture over roast. Bake for another 45 minutes to one hour, until a meat thermometer inserted in the center reads 125 to 130 degrees for medium-rare. Remove from oven; let stand for 15 minutes before slicing. Serve roast with roasted onions, garlic and pan juices, as desired. If desired, garnish with fresh herbs. Serves 8 to 10.

For dark, rich-looking gravy, add a spoonful or two
of brewed coffee. It will add color to pale gravy
but won't affect the flavor.

# Grandma's Best *Christmas* RECIPES

## Apple & Spice Pork Roast

*Sue Klapper*
*Muskego, WI*

*I love serving this delicious roast for weekend family dinners and special occasions. I always get compliments! Don't let the number of ingredients stop you from trying this delicious roast...I'm sure you have most of them in your kitchen. Enjoy!*

3 to 4-lb. boneless pork roast
1 c. applesauce
1/2 c. brown sugar, packed
2 t. vinegar
1 t. mustard
1/4 t. ground cloves

1 T. all-purpose flour
1/4 t. sugar
1/8 t. garlic powder
1/2 t. salt
1/8 t. pepper

Place roast on a wire rack in a shallow roasting pan; set aside. In a small bowl, stir together applesauce, brown sugar, vinegar, mustard and cloves. Set aside half of applesauce mixture; cover and refrigerate the remainder. In another small bowl, combine flour, sugar and seasonings; rub mixture evenly over entire surface of roast. Bake, uncovered, at 350 degrees until a meat thermometer inserted in the center reads 140 degrees. Spoon reserved applesauce mixture over roast. Continue baking until internal temperature is 150 degrees, for a total of one to 1-1/2 hours cooking time. Transfer roast to a serving platter; cover with aluminum foil and let stand for 15 minutes before slicing. Meanwhile, heat chilled applesauce mixture in a small saucepan until boiling; boil for one minute. Spoon warm applesauce mixture over sliced pork and serve. Makes 8 servings.

Have little ones write down all the reasons they love their grandparents and present the list at Christmas. Handwritten on special paper and framed, it'll make a truly meaningful gift.

# Coming Home for Christmas Dinner

## Grandma's Meatballs

*Beth Miller*
*Rochester, IN*

*My grandma made this recipe often when her children and grandchildren visited for Sunday dinner. It has been passed down through three generations. My 11-year-old grandson has made it.... that's generation number four! It's an easy recipe to put together and can be doubled to feed more family members.*

1-1/2 lbs. ground beef
3/4 c. old-fashioned oats,
   uncooked
1 c. milk
1 onion, diced
1/2 t. salt

1/2 t. pepper
1 c. catsup
1/2 c. water
2 T. brown sugar, packed
2 T. Worcestershire sauce
2 T. vinegar

Mix beef, oats, milk, onion, salt and pepper in a large bowl. Scoop into meatballs, slightly less than 1/4-cup each; arrange in a lightly greased 8"x8" baking pan. For sauce, mix together catsup, water, brown sugar, Worcestershire sauce and vinegar. Spoon over meatballs. Bake, uncovered, at 350 degrees for 1-1/2 hours. Makes 6 servings.

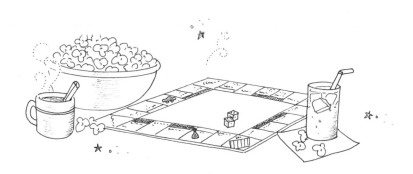

Stay in on a snowy night! Fill the table with lots of tasty snacks and pull out a favorite board game or two. What fun for the entire family!

# Grandma's Best
# Christmas
## RECIPES

## Gran's Glazed Roast Chicken

*Nancy Wise*
*Little Rock, AR*

*I've had this recipe for years and serve it often with homemade cornbread stuffing on the side. It reminds me of my grandmother's wonderful roast chicken.*

3 to 4-lb. roasting chicken
1 to 2 T. oil
salt and pepper to taste

1/2 c. peach preserves
1 T. butter, melted
1 T. lemon juice

Place chicken on a wire rack in an ungreased roasting pan. Brush lightly with oil; season with salt and pepper. Bake, uncovered, at 375 degrees for one hour and 15 minutes. Meanwhile, combine preserves, melted butter and lemon juice in a small bowl; spoon over chicken. Return to oven. Bake another 15 minutes, or until golden and a meat thermometer reads 165 degrees. Remove chicken to a platter; let stand for 10 minutes. Slice and serve. Makes 4 to 6 servings.

## Snowy-Day Chicken Pot Pie

*Linda Peterson*
*Mason, MI*

*My grandma made this and it was so delicious. I asked for the recipe, and was very surprised by how easy it is.*

2  10-3/4 oz. cans cream of
   chicken soup
1 c. chicken broth
16-oz. pkg. frozen mixed
   vegetables, thawed

3 c. cooked chicken, diced
1 c. all-purpose flour
1 c. milk
1/2 c. butter, melted

In a large bowl, whisk together chicken soup and chicken broth; fold in vegetables and chicken. Spoon into a greased 13"x9" baking pan; set aside. For crust, mix remaining ingredients and spoon over chicken mixture. Bake, uncovered, at 400 degrees for one hour, or until bubbly and crust is golden. Serves 6.

# Coming Home for Christmas Dinner

## Our Holiday Roast Goose

*Beckie Apple*
*Grannis, AR*

*Years ago, my mom and my two sisters decided to try roasting
a goose for our holiday meal. We had no experience with it,
but found it really easy to do. Our family loved it!*

8 to 10-lb. roasting goose,
  thawed if frozen
3 tart apples, halved and cored
6 stalks celery, cut into 5-inch
  sticks

3 lemons, halved
1 onion, cut into quarters
1 T. dried sage
1/2 c. butter, room temperature
salt and pepper to taste

Remove giblets from goose; pat goose dry with paper towels and place
in a large roasting pan. Insert apples, celery, lemons, onion and sage
into cavity of goose. Rub butter over the outside of goose; season with
salt and pepper. Cover with aluminum foil. Bake at 300 degrees for
2 hours. Uncover; bake at 350 degrees for 45 minutes, or until a meat
thermometer inserted in the thickest part reads 165 to 170 degrees.
Remove goose to a platter; discard fruits and vegetables. Let stand for
20 to 30 minutes before carving. Makes 8 to 10 servings.

Set a potted rosemary wreath in a kitchen window...oh-so handy
for adding flavorful fresh sprigs to roasting meats and vegetables.
Tie on tiny red bows to contrast with the evergreen foliage. Sweet!

# Grandma's Best Christmas RECIPES

## Grandma Shaffer's Sunday Stew

*Marcia Shaffer*
*Conneaut Lake, PA*

*With this recipe, you can go to Sunday School and church, and have enough time to set the table when you get home. My dad always told us kids, if you don't stay for church after Sunday School, it's like missing your dessert after a good meal!*

2 lbs. stew beef cubes
3 carrots, peeled and sliced
3 potatoes, peeled and quartered
2 onions, sliced
1 yellow turnip, cubed

10-3/4 oz. can tomato soup
3/4 c. water
salt and pepper to taste
1 bay leaf

Combine all ingredients in a lightly greased 3-quart heavy casserole dish with a close-fitting lid. Mix well. Cover and bake at 275 degrees for 5 hours. Discard bay leaf and serve. Makes 6 to 8 servings.

Stir up some memories...invite Grandma & Grandpa to read Christmas stories to little ones and share holiday stories from their childhood.

# Coming Home for Christmas Dinner

## One-Pot Pork Chop Dinner

*Patricia Damers*
*Smithtown, NY*

*Like an old friend, this recipe is simple, warm and comforting.*

1-1/2 T. oil
4 bone-in pork chops,
   1/2-inch thick
6 to 8 new potatoes, peeled
   and halved
4 small carrots, peeled and cut
   into 2-inch pieces

10-3/4 oz. can tomato soup
1/2 c. water
1 t. Worcestershire sauce
1/2 t. caraway seed or dried
   oregano
1/2 t. salt

Heat oil in a large skillet over medium heat. Add pork chops and brown on both sides; drain. Add remaining ingredients; stir well. Cover and simmer for 45 minutes, or until pork chops and vegetables are tender. Makes 4 servings.

## Grandma's Goulash

*Joyce Page*
*Newport, PA*

*My grandmother always made this tasty dish whenever I spent a few days visiting with her and Grandpa. It is now a favorite of my own family...I like to double the recipe so that we will have leftovers! Serve with hot garlic bread.*

8-oz. pkg. spaghetti, uncooked
1 lb. ground beef
1/3 c. onion, chopped
10-3/4 oz. can vegetable soup
1 c. catsup

1/4 t. chili powder
1-1/2 t. salt
1/4 t. pepper
1 c. grated Parmesan cheese,
   divided

Cook spaghetti according to package directions; drain. Brown beef with onion in a skillet over medium heat; drain. Combine remaining ingredients except Parmesan cheese in a bowl; add to beef mixture. Add cooked spaghetti and mix well. Transfer to a greased 2-quart casserole dish; sprinkle with 1/2 cup Parmesan cheese. Cover with aluminum foil and bake at 350 degrees for 30 minutes. Remove foil; bake for an additional 10 minutes. Serve with remaining cheese. Makes 6 servings.

## Aunt Sherry's Chicken Braid

*Jennifer Dorward*
*Winder, GA*

*This recipe was from my Aunt Sherry, who passed away much too soon! She taught my mom how to make it, and all these years later it's still a family favorite. We make it and think fondly of Aunt Sherry and her love for us and for good food. We enjoy this with a mixture of greens for a nice salad. It's delicious!*

1 broccoli crown
3-lb. deli rotisserie chicken
1 c. shredded Cheddar cheese
1 c. mayonnaise
1/2 c. sour cream
2 T. garlic powder

1 T. onion powder
salt and pepper to taste
2 8-oz. tubes refrigerated
  crescent rolls
Garnish: beaten egg or
  melted butter

Bring a saucepan of water to a boil over high heat. Add broccoli and cook until soft; drain well, chop and cool. Meanwhile, shred chicken into a large bowl, discarding skin and bones. Add broccoli, cheese, mayonnaise, sour cream and seasonings; mix well. Unroll both tubes of crescent rolls and press together on a baking sheet, forming a large rectangle. Spoon chicken mixture down the center. Cut the exposed dough on both sides into one-inch strips. Lift each strip on the right; twist it a few times and lay it over chicken mixture. Repeat with each strip on the left and lay it across the right strip, forming an X. Proceed until all strips are twisted and crossed or braided down the center. Brush with beaten egg or melted butter. Bake at 375 degrees for 25 to 30 minutes, until golden. Slice and serve. Makes 7 to 8 servings.

If it's been too long since you've visited with good friends, why not host a casual holiday get-together? Potlucks are so easy to plan...everyone brings along their favorite dish to share. It's all about food, fun and fellowship!

# Coming Home for Christmas Dinner

## Aunt Jo's Famous Turkey Mega Muffins

Marcia Jackson
Bolingbrook, IL

*My Aunt Jo Ann was a wonderful cook. Besides her everyday job, she was the weekly cook and head of a kitchen staff for a large Baptist church in Ennis, Texas. She is part of the reason I love to cook! I sure do miss her. Serve this with mashed potatoes, gravy and a couple more veggies...it'll taste just like a mini Thanksgiving Day. Chicken can be used as well. Rotisserie chicken is awesome!*

4 eggs, beaten
2 c. whipping cream or
　half-and-half
6-oz. pkg. cornbread
　stuffing mix

2 c. cooked turkey, cut into
　bite-size cubes
Optional: 1/2 c. sweetened dried
　cranberries

In a large bowl, whisk together eggs and cream or half-and-half. Add stuffing mix and toss to mix well; fold in turkey or chicken and cranberries. Let stand for a few minutes. Lightly grease 6 to 8 Texas-size extra-large muffin cups, or 10 to 12 regular muffin cups. Spoon stuffing mixture into muffin cups, filling 2/3 full. Bake at 350 degrees for 25 to 30 minutes, until centers are set. Let stand for 5 minutes before removing muffins from pan. Serves 6 to 8.

A loving gift for your child straight from the heart...assemble a recipe box with all of Grandma's favorite recipes. Add new recipes each year along with funny little notes and sayings. A warm, wonderful gift to grow right along with your child... truly a box full of memories!

# Grandma's Best *Christmas* RECIPES

## Baked Teriyaki Chicken

*Marlene Darnell*
*Newport Beach, CA*

*Grandma loved her trips to Hawaii. She made this recipe to remind herself of them. Serve with roasted sweet potatoes and grilled or broiled fresh pineapple...yum!*

10 to 12 boneless, skinless
   chicken thighs
1/2 c. soy sauce
1/4 c. cider vinegar
1 T. cold water

1/2 c. sugar
1 T. cornstarch
1 clove garlic, minced
1/2 t. ground ginger
1/4 t. pepper

Arrange chicken thighs in a well-greased 13"x9" baking pan; set aside. Combine remaining ingredients in a small saucepan over low heat. Simmer, stirring often, until sauce thickens and bubbles. Brush sauce over chicken; turn chicken over and brush again. Bake, uncovered, at 375 degrees for 30 minutes. Turn chicken over. Bake for another 30 minutes, brushing often with sauce, or until glazed and juices run clear when pierced. Makes 5 to 6 servings, 2 pieces each.

A Christmas family party...we know of nothing
in nature more delightful! There seems a magic
in the very name of Christmas.
—Charles Dickens

# Coming Home for Christmas Dinner

## Turkey-Asparagus Bake

*Sharlene Reid*
*British Columbia, Canada*

*This is a wonderful way to use up leftover turkey after Thanksgiving or Christmas. It's been a family favorite for many years. Serve with cranberry sauce on the side...delicious.*

1 lb. fresh asparagus, cooked
    and cut into 1-inch pieces
4 to 6 generous slices roast
    turkey, cut into bite-size
    pieces
10-3/4 oz. can cream of chicken
    or celery soup

1/2 c. whole milk or light cream
1/2 t. dried marjoram or poultry
    seasoning
1/2 c. grated Parmesan cheese

Spread 1/3 of asparagus in a greased 13"x9" baking pan; arrange 1/3 of turkey on top. Repeat layering, making 2 more layers; set aside. In a saucepan, whisk together soup and milk or cream over low heat until just blended. Stir in seasoning; spoon over turkey mixture. Sprinkle with Parmesan cheese. Bake, uncovered, at 350 degrees for 30 minutes, or until hot and bubbly. Makes 4 servings.

## Chicken Casserole

*Roberta Simpkins*
*Mentor on the Lake, OH*

*I remember going to my grandma's house and having this dish with all my cousins. We could hardly wait to gather at the kiddie table and have dinner! When I make it now, I serve with fresh green beans and a large garden salad...yum!*

4 to 6 c. cooked chicken, cubed
10-3/4 oz. can cream of
    chicken soup
10-3/4 oz. can cream of
    celery soup

2/3 c. sour cream
2 6-oz. pkgs. chicken-flavored
    dressing mix

Spread chicken cubes in a lightly greased 3-quart casserole dish. Blend together soups and sour cream; spoon over chicken. Prepare dressing according to package directions; spoon over soup mixture. Bake, uncovered, at 325 degrees for one hour, or until heated through. Serves 6 to 8.

# Grandma's Best *Christmas* RECIPES

## Christmas Crab Cakes

*Paula Marchesi*
*Auburn, PA*

*Growing up on the eastern end of Long Island, New York, I love all sorts of seafood, especially at Christmas. It brings back lots of good memories. We used to go fishing, catch crabs in the bay on a moonlit night, go clamming when it was low tide, and the list goes on & on. So it's only right that I serve seafood on Christmas Eve. These crab cakes are one of my favorites...crisp on the outside, tender on the inside, exactly how I grew up eating them. They're quick & easy to make and simply delicious.*

1 egg, beaten
1 T. mayonnaise
1 t. Dijon mustard
1 t. dry mustard
1 t. fresh parsley, minced
1 t. seafood seasoning
1/2 t. salt
1/4 t. pepper

1 lb. lump crabmeat, drained
  and flaked
1-1/2 c. white bread, and finely
  crumbled
3 T. canola oil
Garnish: garlic butter sauce,
  tartar sauce or cocktail sauce

In a large bowl, combine egg, mayonnaise, mustards, parsley and seasonings. Mix until blended. Fold in crabmeat until well coated. Gently stir in bread crumbs. Shape into 12 patties, each 1/2-inch thick. In a large skillet, heat oil over medium-high heat. Add crab cakes, working in batches; cook for 2 to 3 minutes on each side, until darkly golden. Remove to paper towels to drain; pat with paper towels and arrange on a serving platter. Serve with desired sauce. Makes 12 servings.

Fresh Salad Dressing
½ olive oil cup
⅓ cup fresh lemon juice
1 Tab. Dijon Mustard
Salt & Pepper to taste
SHAKE!

A crisp green salad with a lemony dressing goes well with seafood dishes. Simply shake up 1/2 cup olive oil, 1/3 cup fresh lemon juice and a tablespoon of Dijon mustard in a small jar and chill to blend.

# Coming Home for Christmas Dinner

## Scallops with Rosemary & Almonds

*Irene Robinson*
*Cincinnati, OH*

*Super-easy and quick for an elegant holiday meal with friends.*
*Serve with baked potatoes with sour cream, steamed*
*asparagus and warm rolls...delicious!*

1 lb. sea scallops
3 T. dry bread crumbs
1 T. fresh rosemary, minced

1 T. Dijon mustard
1 T. butter, melted
1/4 c. sliced almonds

Rinse scallops and pat dry. Coat well with bread crumbs and divide
among 4 buttered ramekins. Combine remaining ingredients in a cup;
divide evenly among ramekins. Bake, uncovered, at 350 degrees for
20 minutes, or until scallops are done. Serves 4.

Host a Christmas Eve buffet without the fuss. Divide
the meal into courses and let guests choose a course
to bring...spend less time in the kitchen and more
with family & friends!

# Grandma's Best *Christmas* RECIPES

## Cajun-Spiced Black-Eyed Pea & Cabbage Stew

*Sherry Sheehan*
*Evensville, TN*

*Every year, I try a different New Year's Day recipe. This year, I created one to fit our family's dietary needs. Cooking in a slow cooker means we can spend New Year's Day watching the parades and football games we enjoy on television. I like to use a slow-cooker liner for easier clean-up. Serve with cornbread.*

2  15.8-oz. cans black-eyed
    peas, drained
10-oz. can diced tomatoes with
    green chiles
6 c. cabbage, coarsely chopped

13-1/2 oz. pkg. andouille
    smoked pork sausage, sliced
2 c. chicken broth
1/2 t. dried, minced garlic
1/2 t. Cajun seasoning

Combine all ingredients in a 6-quart slow cooker; mix gently. Cover and cook on low setting for 6 to 8 hours, until cabbage is tender. Stir again and serve. Makes 6 to 8 servings.

Fill a big Mason jar with Grandma's favorite hard candies and place it in the center of the dining table...don't forget to count them first! Ask everyone to guess how many candies are in the jar. Send the jar home with the person whose guess is the closest.

# Coming Home for Christmas Dinner

## Corned Beef & Cabbage

*Barbara Klein*
*Newburgh, IN*

*I love to serve this on New Year's Day...it's a delicious cold-weather dinner! Great served with a hearty brioche bread.*

4-lb. corned beef brisket with
    spice packet
1 onion, quartered
3 carrots, peeled and cut into
    large chunks
3 stalks celery, cut into
    2-inch pieces

1 t. salt
12 c. water
2 lbs. new redskin potatoes,
    halved if desired
8-oz. pkg. baby carrots
1 small head cabbage, cut into
    8 wedges

In a large Dutch oven, combine corned beef and spice packet contents, onion, carrots, celery and salt. Pour water over all. Bring to a simmer over medium-high heat, skimming off any foam that rises to the surface. Reduce heat to low. Cover and simmer for about 3 hours, until beef is almost fork-tender. Add potatoes and simmer, uncovered, until potatoes are almost tender, about 30 minutes more. Add carrots; arrange cabbage on top of and around beef. Cover and continue simmering another 20 to 30 minutes, until vegetables are tender. Serves 6 to 8.

Make it easy on yourself when planning holiday dinners...stick to tried & true recipes! You'll find your guests are just as happy with simple comfort foods as with the most elegant gourmet meal.

# *Grandma's Best* *Christmas* RECIPES

## Grandma Judy's Spaghetti Casserole

*Andrea Heyart*
*Savannah, TX*

*For as long as I can remember, my Grandma Judy's spaghetti casserole has been served at family gatherings. It's one of the first recipes each person in our family learns to make. It also freezes really well, so it's a perfect dish to make ahead and pull out when company arrives. One pan for the grown-ups, and one for the kids' table!*

2 lbs. ground beef
16-oz. pkg. spaghetti, uncooked
1/2 c. butter, melted
2 c. Italian-seasoned dry
   bread crumbs

Separately prepare sauces; set aside. Meanwhile, brown beef in a skillet over medium heat; drain. Cook spaghetti according to package directions; drain. Toss melted butter with bread crumbs; set aside. To assemble: in one greased 13"x9" baking pan and one greased 8"x8" baking pan, layer half each of cooked spaghetti, Red Sauce, browned beef, Cheese Sauce and bread crumbs. Repeat layering. Bake, uncovered, at 350 degrees for 30 minutes, or until hot and bubbly. Serves 12.

### Red Sauce:

3 green peppers, diced
2 yellow onions, diced
6 T. butter
2 8-oz. cans tomato sauce

In a large saucepan over medium heat, sauté green peppers and onions in butter until peppers are soft and onions are translucent. Add tomato sauce; simmer over medium-low heat for 40 minutes.

### Cheese Sauce:

1/2 c. butter
1/2 c. all-purpose flour
4 c. milk
16-oz. pkg. pasteurized process
   cheese, cubed

Melt butter in a large saucepan over medium-low heat. Stir in flour to form a paste. Add milk and cheese; cook and stir until smooth and cheese has melted.

# Festive
# Open House
# Appetizers

# Grandma's Best *Christmas* RECIPES

## Family-Favorite Swedish Meatballs

*Gail Kelsey*
*Mesa, AZ*

*Christmas wouldn't be Christmas without these delicious Swedish meatballs! This recipe comes from my husband's Swedish family and is loved by all. We serve them as a cocktail appetizer, or you can make a gravy from the broth and serve them over noodles.*

1 lb. boneless beef
1 lb. boneless veal or turkey
1/2 lb. boneless pork
4 slices bread, torn
3/4 c. whole milk
2 eggs, lightly beaten
1 onion, finely chopped

1 clove garlic, mashed
1/8 t. nutmeg
1/8 t. allspice
2 t. salt
1/4 t. pepper
1/2 c. shortening
3 c. beef broth, heated

Have the meats ground well together; add to a large bowl and set aside. In a small bowl, make a paste of bread and milk; add to meat mixture along with remaining ingredients except shortening and beef broth. Stir until stiff; scoop into one-inch balls and let stand on wax paper for 30 minutes. Melt shortening in a skillet over medium heat. Working in batches, cook meatballs until just done; do not overcook. Arrange meatballs on a rimmed baking sheet; pour hot broth over all. Bake, uncovered, at 350 degrees for 30 minutes. Serve meatballs with or without broth. Makes about 14 servings.

Silently, like thoughts that come and go,
the snowflakes fall, each one a gem.
– William Hamilton Gibson

# Festive Open House Appetizers

## Nonnie's Rumaki

*Kristen Mitchell*
*Bartlett, IL*

*This is a classic Christmas Eve hors d'oeuvre our family has enjoyed since the 1950s. Unique variations include adding chicken livers, asparagus, or other interesting foods to be wrapped in bacon.*

1 c. catsup
1/2 c. brown sugar
3 T. Worcestershire sauce
1/2 t. garlic powder

4 8-oz. cans whole water
chestnuts, drained
1 lb. thick cut bacon, cut into
2-inch pieces

In a small bowl, combine catsup, brown sugar, Worcestershire sauce and garlic powder; mix well. Cover and refrigerate. Wrap each water chestnut in bacon and secure with a wooden toothpick. Set on an ungreased baking sheet, one inch apart. Cover loosely with aluminum foil. Bake at 425 degrees for 20 to 30 minutes, until bacon is 3/4 cooked, watching closely. Uncover; drain excess drippings from pan and flip over. Top each chestnut with a generous dollop of chilled catsup mixture. Reduce oven temperature to 375 degrees; return to oven for another 15 minutes, or until golden and bacon is crisp. Serve warm on a decorative tray. Makes about 2 dozen.

Host a nostalgic Christmas party for family & friends! Decorate the table with shiny bright ornaments and tinsel garland, serve up all those yummy party foods like Grandma used to make, and play all those classic old Christmas records we cherish from the 50s and 60s. Sure to be a wonderful time!

# Grandma's Best Christmas RECIPES

## Treva's Polish Mistakes

*Teri Bishop-Johnson*
*Austin, MN*

*This was originally my Grandma Treva's recipe, and I've tweaked it to my liking. It is by far one of my favorite appetizers.*

1 lb. ground hot pork sausage
1 lb. ground beef
1/2 c. white onion, chopped
1 T. Worcestershire sauce
1 t. dried oregano
1/2 t. garlic salt

salt and pepper to taste
1 lb. pasteurized process
   cheese, cubed
12-oz. pkg. pumpernickel rye
   party loaf

In a large skillet over medium heat, cook sausage, beef and onion, Worcestershire sauce and seasonings until browned; drain. Fold in cheese cubes; simmer until cheese is melted. To serve, spoon onto rye slices. Serves 6 to 8.

## Mediterranean Broiled Sandwich

*Wendy Meadows*
*Spring Hill, FL*

*I inherited my grandmother's recipe box. Every so often, I look for a recipe of hers that reminds me of sitting at her table as a kid during a snowstorm. This is one she served at card night and I was always tasked with chopping the olives. She figured if I was busy chopping them, I wouldn't eat too many of them!*

4 slices bread
4 slices bacon, crisply cooked
   and crumbled
1 c. shredded Swiss cheese

1/4 c. mayonnaise
1/4 c. chopped black olives,
   drained
2 T. green onions, chopped

Toast bread; set aside. In a bowl, mix together remaining ingredients. Spread on toasted bread and place on a broiler pan. Broil for 2 minutes, about 4 inches from heat, until cheese melts. Serve warm. Makes 4 open-face sandwiches.

# *Festive Open House Appetizers*

## Libby's Ham Ball

*Alice Joy Randall*
*Nacogdoches, TX*

*This is my sister-in-law Libby's recipe. I often make it at Christmas for special friends...it is a favorite of my nephew. You'll want to use regular baked ham, not honey ham.*

2 8-oz. pkgs. cream cheese, softened
1 T. mayonnaise-style salad dressing
1 t. lemon juice
Optional: few drops hot pepper sauce

8-oz. pkg. thinly sliced deli-style baked ham
1 small bunch green onions, minced, white part with a little of green part
snack crackers

In a large bowl, combine cream cheese, salad dressing, lemon juice and hot sauce, if using. Beat with an electric mixer on medium speed until creamy; set aside. Chop ham in a food processor and add to cream cheese mixture, reserving some ham for coating the finished ham ball. Add onions to mixture; blend well. With a spatula, mound mixture in the center of a serving platter, smoothing the top and sides. Lightly press reserved chopped ham onto top and sides. Cover and chill. Serve with crackers. Makes 8 servings.

Invite everyone to a tree-trimming party! Play your favorite holiday music and serve lots of tasty snacks. Before you know it, everyone will be in the holiday spirit.

## Toasted Mushroom Rolls

*Laurie White*
*Geneseo, KS*

*My mother was always a participant in the Hutchinson News recipe contest over the holidays...she always was trying out something new on her family. In 1989, this recipe was a winner for Mom, taking second place in Appetizers. We think it's still a winner!*

3/4 lb. mushrooms, finely
   chopped
1/4 c. plus 6 T. butter, divided
1/4 c. all-purpose flour
1 t. salt

1-1/2 c. half-and-half
2 T. fresh chives, minced
1-1/2 t. lemon juice
2 16-oz. loaves sliced sandwich
   bread, crusts trimmed

In a heavy saucepan over medium heat, sauté mushrooms in 6 tablespoons butter for 5 minutes, or until tender. Add flour and salt; stir until smooth. Cook for one minute, stirring constantly. Gradually add half-and-half. Cook over medium heat, stirring constantly, until mixture is thickened and bubbly. Stir in chives and lemon juice; set aside. Roll bread slices with a rolling pin until thin. Spread each bread slice with 2 teaspoons mushroom mixture; roll up jelly-roll fashion. Place rolls, seam-side down, on greased baking sheets. Melt remaining butter and brush over rolls. Bake at 400 degrees for 15 minutes, until golden. Serve hot. Makes 2-1/2 to 3 dozen.

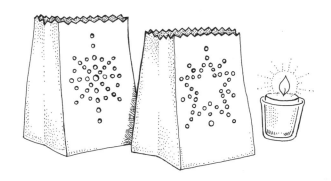

Add a welcoming row of twinkling luminarias along the front walk and your house will be party perfect!

# Festive Open House Appetizers

## Ham & Cheese Pinwheels

*Marian Forck*
*Chamois, MO*

*Tess is my daughter Sarah's mother-in-law. We are so blessed that we all get along and can have our family get-togethers. With Sarah and her husband Aaron being only children, we love that their grandparents can get together as One Big Happy Family.*

8-oz. container whipped
   cream cheese
1 T. ranch salad dressing mix

1 clove garlic, minced
8 10-inch flour tortillas
8 thin slices deli baked ham

Combine cream cheese, dressing mix and garlic in a bowl; blend well and spread over tortillas. Layer with ham slices; roll up tightly and wrap in plastic wrap. Refrigerate for 2 hours. Cut into one-inch slices; arrange on a serving plate. Serves 8.

Bring in a vintage light-up snowman in from the yard
to share the party fun. Tucked in the corner,
he'll spread Christmas cheer.

# *Grandma's Best*
# *Christmas*
## RECIPES

## Christmas Punch

*Ann Turner*
*Garner, NC*

*My great-aunt and my mother used to make this unusual punch for Christmas and other special occasions. The bright red and green cubes looked so festive...it was always a hit at parties! I like to keep a few of each flavor of ice cubes in the freezer to make my own single-serving punch with a can of ginger ale.*

0.13-oz. pkg. unsweetened
    cherry drink mix
0.13-oz. unsweetened lemon-
    lime drink mix

2 2-liter bottles ginger ale,
    chilled

Prepare cherry drink mix according to package instructions. Pour beverage into ice cube trays; place in freezer and freeze until solid. Repeat with lemon-lime drink mix. Transfer frozen ice cubes in separate one-gallon freezer bags, one for cherry and one for lemon-lime. Store in freezer. At serving time, add some of each flavor of frozen ice cubes to a punch bowl or pitcher. Add chilled ginger ale. Throughout the party, add more ice cubes and more ginger ale as needed. Serves 16.

Tie tiny Christmas ornaments onto stemmed glasses
with ribbon bows...so festive!

# Festive Open House Appetizers

## Aunt Tish's Pineapple Cheese Ball

*Monica Britt*
*Fairdale, WV*

*This is one of my family's favorite appetizers, especially at the holidays. I got the recipe years ago from my Aunt Tish.*

2  8-oz. pkgs. cream cheese, softened
8-oz. can crushed pineapple, drained
2 T. onion, minced
1/4 c. green pepper, finely chopped
1 c. pecans, finely chopped
favorite crackers

In a large bowl, blend cream cheese, crushed pineapple, onion and green pepper. Form into a ball. Roll in chopped pecans, coating entire surface. For the best flavor, cover and chill for 8 hours or overnight before serving. Serve with crackers. Makes 12 servings.

## Olive Cheese Ball

*Shirley Howie*
*Foxboro, MA*

*I have been making this recipe for family get-togethers for many years now. It has become a favorite on New Year's Eve!*

8-oz. pkg. cream cheese, softened
8-oz. pkg. crumbled blue cheese
1/4 c. butter, softened
1 T. onion, finely chopped
2/3 c. green olives with pimentos, well drained and chopped
1/3 c. chopped walnuts
assorted crackers

Mix together cheeses and butter until well blended. Stir in onion and olives. Chill slightly; form into a ball. Cover and chill well. Roll ball in chopped walnuts, coating well. Serve with assorted crackers. Makes 3 cups.

Rosemary sprigs and cranberries arranged to resemble holly add a festive touch to holiday platters.

# Grandma's Best
## *Christmas*
### RECIPES

## Grandma's Marinated Shrimp

*Paula Marchesi*
*Auburn, PA*

*Dress up any holiday gathering with this tasty shrimp recipe. It's quick & easy to make...you'll even have time to enjoy your guests!*

3/4 c. water
1/2 c. red wine vinegar
1/4 c. olive oil
1 clove garlic, minced
3/4 t. fresh oregano, minced
3/4 t. fresh thyme, minced
3/4 t. salt
1/4 t. pepper

1-1/2 lbs. cooked jumbo shrimp, peeled
14-oz. can artichoke hearts in water, drained, rinsed and halved
1/2 lb. small mushrooms, trimmed and halved

In a large plastic zipping bag, combine water, vinegar, oil, garlic, herbs, salt and pepper. Add shrimp, artichokes and mushrooms to bag. Seal bag and turn to coat. Refrigerate for 8 hours or overnight, turning bag occasionally. Drain; transfer to a serving bowl. Makes 8 servings.

Bring a bit of retro to the holiday kitchen...
tie on a vintage Christmas apron!

# *Festive Open House Appetizers*

## Cranberry Feta Pinwheels

*Lisa Rischar*
*Cedar Lake, IN*

*This sweet and salty appetizer makes a great Christmas treat.*
*I like to arrange the pinwheels on a serving plate in the shape*
*of a Christmas tree...very festive!*

8-oz. pkg. cream cheese,
   softened
3/4 c. sweetened dried
   cranberries

3/4 c. crumbled feta cheese
1/4 c. green onions, chopped
4  10-inch flour tortillas

In a bowl, mix together all ingredients except tortillas. Spread mixture evenly on tortillas. Roll up tightly. Wrap in plastic wrap; refrigerate for one hour. Cut each roll into 3 pieces; arrange on a serving plate. Makes 12 servings.

Share the greetings of the season! Clip Christmas cards to
a pine garland and hang it across bookcase shelves.

# Grandma's Best *Christmas* RECIPES

## Parmesan Pizza Snacks

*Karen Wilson*
*Defiance, OH*

*I'm always looking for recipes that my grandchildren would like. These pizza snacks are a winner!*

13.8-oz. tube refrigerated
    pizza dough
20 slices pepperoni
5 mozzarella sticks, each cut
    into 4 pieces

2 T. butter, melted and cooled
    slightly
1/4 c. grated Parmesan cheese
1 c. marinara sauce, warmed

Unroll pizza dough; cut into 20 equal squares. Press each square into a 2-1/2 inch square. Top each square with one pepperoni slice and one piece of cheese. Wrap dough around fillings; press edges to seal. Dip each roll in melted butter; arrange seam-side down in a greased 9"x9" baking pan. Sprinkle rolls with Parmesan cheese. Bake at 375 degrees for 18 to 22 minutes, until golden. Serve warm with marinara sauce. Serves 10, 2 pieces each.

## Warm Christmas Punch

*Andrea Heyart*
*Savannah, TX*

*This spiced drink makes the whole house smell like Christmas! It's a variation on my grandmother's holiday punch recipe.*

64-oz. bottle fruit punch
64-oz. bottle cranberry juice
4 c. pineapple juice

2 4-inch cinnamon sticks
4 whole cloves

Add all ingredients to a 5-quart slow cooker, enclosing spices in a spice bag, if desired. Cover and cook on high setting for 3 to 4 hours. Discard spices; serve hot. Makes 15 to 20 servings.

Sparkly sticks of rock candy are
fun for stirring hot beverages.

# Festive Open House Appetizers

## Mom's Cheddar Cheese Ball
*Heather Bartlett*
*Marietta, GA*

*My mom made this cheese ball for us every Christmas while we were growing up. Now I make it and it is loved by all. Serve with your choice of crackers.*

16-oz. pkg. shredded Cheddar
   cheese
8-oz. pkg. cream cheese,
   softened
1/3 c. mayonnaise

1 t. Worcestershire sauce
1/8 t. onion powder
1/8 t. garlic powder
6-oz. pkg. real bacon bits

In a large bowl, mix together all ingredients except bacon bits. Form into 2 to 3 balls. Spread bacon bits on a plate and roll the balls around, coating well. Chill until ready to serve. Makes 12 to 15 servings.

For an easy yet elegant appetizer, try a cheese platter. Choose a soft cheese, a hard cheese and a semi-soft or crumbly cheese. Add a basket of crisp crackers, crusty baguettes and some sliced apples or pears. Arrange it all on your favorite vintage tray. So simple, yet sure to please guests!

## Warm Family Dip

*Jeannie Stone*
*Nova Scotia, Canada*

*Over the years, whenever we have a special event like decorating the Christmas tree or watching a special movie together, our family always loves to sit back and share a warm dip. The great thing about it? Sometimes it's chicken, sometimes it's seafood, sometimes it's vegetarian...but the dip itself never changes. You can add whatever you like, or whatever is left over in the fridge. Now the family asks for it whenever we all get together.*

8-oz. pkg. cream cheese, softened
1/2 c. mayonnaise
1/2 c. sour cream
2 T. French or Catalina salad dressing
1 T. mustard
2 c. cooked chicken, turkey, crabmeat, lobster or mushrooms, chopped
1/2 c. celery, chopped
1/2 c. carrot, peeled and shredded
1/2 c. cracker crumbs
1/4 c. shredded Parmesan cheese
crackers or tortilla chips

In a large bowl, combine cream cheese, mayonnaise, sour cream, salad dressing and mustard. Beat with an electric mixer on medium speed for 4 minutes, or until light and fluffy. Mix in meat or mushrooms, celery and carrot; spoon into a lightly greased 2-quart casserole dish. Top with cracker crumbs and Parmesan cheese. Bake, uncovered, at 350 degrees for 35 minutes, or until hot and bubbly. Serve with crackers or tortilla chips. Makes 6 servings.

'Tis the season...hang a sprig of mistletoe
in the doorway!

# Festive Open House Appetizers

## Holiday Cranberry Salsa

*Sonia Daily*
*Charlotte, NC*

*This is a great appetizer for Thanksgiving or Christmas...just set it out for everyone to nibble on as they wait for dinner. A food processor makes it easy. Serve with tortilla chips.*

2 12-oz. pkgs. fresh cranberries
1 Granny Smith apple, cored and
   cut into chunks
1/2 c. red onion, cut into chunks

1 c. fresh cilantro, stems
   removed
1-1/4 c. sugar
juice of 1 lime

With a food processor or a sharp knife, finely chop cranberries, apple, onion and cilantro. Combine all ingredients in a large bowl; toss to mix. Cover and refrigerate at least 2 to 3 hours to allow flavors to blend, or overnight for the best flavor. Serves 12.

Spoon your favorite secret-recipe dip or spread into a vintage canning jar...an ideal hostess gift. Add a box of crisp crackers and tie on a spreader with a pretty ribbon. Sure to be appreciated!

## Grandma Gladys's Christmas Caramel Corn

*Gladys Kielar*
*Whitehouse, OH*

*This caramel corn makes a wonderful holiday gift to give*
*to neighbors and friends...it's a great party treat, too!*

8 c. popped popcorn
1-1/2 c. chopped almonds,
   cashews or pecans
2 7-oz. pkgs. dried fruit bits
1 c. brown sugar, packed

1/2 c. sugar
2/3 c. butter
1/3 c. light corn syrup
1/2 t. baking soda
1/2 t. vanilla extract

Place popcorn on a large rimmed baking sheet; discard any unpopped kernels. Add nuts and dried fruit to popcorn; mix gently and set aside. In a heavy saucepan over medium heat, combine sugars, butter and corn syrup. Bring to a boil, stirring often. Cook and stir for about 15 minutes, until mixture is golden. Remove from heat. Stir in baking soda and vanilla; spoon over popcorn mixture. Stir gently to coat well. Bake, uncovered, at 300 degrees for 15 minutes. Stir; continue baking 5 minutes. Transfer mixture to aluminum foil and cool thoroughly. Store in an airtight container, breaking up any chunks. Makes one gallon.

Campfires, toasted marshmallows and ghost stories are
a classic combination. Why not whip up a batch of s'mores
to snack on and gather the family by the fireplace for
a reading of *A Christmas Carol*?

# Festive Open House Appetizers

## Fruit Salsa with Cinnamon Chips

*Carolyn Deckard*
*Bedford, IN*

*My daughter Debbie started making this tasty salsa to serve with cinnamon chips. Now it's a family tradition!*

2 Golden Delicious apples, peeled, cored and chopped
2 kiwi fruit, peeled and chopped
1 lb. strawberries, hulled and chopped

1/2 lb. raspberries, chopped
2 T. sugar
1 T. brown sugar, packed
3 T. favorite fruit preserves

Combine all ingredients in a large bowl; mix thoroughly. Cover and chill for at least 15 minutes. Serve salsa with Cinnamon Chips. Serves 10.

### Cinnamon Chips:

10 10-inch flour tortillas, cut into wedges

2 T. cinnamon
1 c. sugar

Arrange tortilla wedges in a single layer on a large baking sheet. Spray one side of each wedge with non-stick butter-flavored spray. Combine cinnamon and sugar in a bowl. Sprinkle wedges with desired amount of cinnamon-sugar; spray again. Bake at 350 degrees for 8 to 10 minutes. Allow to cool for 15 minutes before serving.

Send out party invitations early, so family & friends can save time on their busy holiday calendars.

# Grandma's Best *Christmas* RECIPES

## Christmas Day Wassail

*Donna Wilson*
*Maryville, TN*

*This is our family's traditional hot drink every Christmas day. It smells so good simmering in the slow cooker, as we open gifts and get the dinner prepared for the big meal. Now that a few of my kids are on their own, they request this recipe too.*

46-oz. bottle apple juice
12-oz. can frozen orange,
   pineapple or apple juice
   concentrate, thawed
2 c. water

1/2 c. brown sugar, packed
1 whole orange, cut into wedges
   or slices
1 t. whole cloves
2 4-inch cinnamon sticks

In a 4-quart slow cooker, combine fruit juices, water and brown sugar; stir well. Stud orange wedges or slices with whole cloves. Add oranges and cinnamon sticks to slow cooker. Cover and cook on low setting for 4 hours. Turn to warm setting for serving. Makes 12 servings.

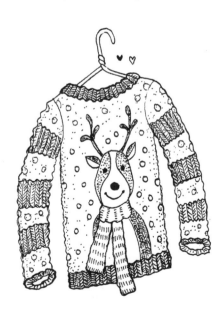

Have an ugly Christmas sweater party! Invite everyone to wear their favorite sweater, and have everyone vote for their favorite, with a small prize for the winner. Fun for all!

# Festive Open House Appetizers

## Creamy Crab Cheese Dip

*Sandy Ward*
*Anderson, IN*

*Such a good dip for special occasions! Wonderful for celebrating Christmas or New Year's Eve. Serve with assorted crackers.*

8-oz. pkg. cream cheese, softened
1/4 c. mascarpone cheese, softened
8-oz. pkg. lump crabmeat, drained and flaked

3 T. green onions, finely chopped
2 T. Worcestershire sauce
1 T. lemon juice
1/2 t. garlic powder
1/4 t. paprika

Combine all ingredients in a large bowl; mix well. Cover and chill at least one hour before serving. Makes 6 to 8 servings.

## Mom's Best Easy Spread

*Lynn Vance*
*Tucson, AZ*

*Mom made this every holiday...with only two ingredients, why not! Serve with Melba toast, rye crisps or any kind of snack cracker.*

8-oz. pkg. cream cheese, softened

1/4 onion, any kind, finely minced

In a large bowl, beat cream cheese with an electric mixer on medium speed until fluffy. Fold in onion. Mound on a small saucer or in a small bowl and serve. Makes 20 servings.

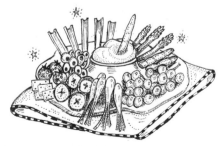

A relish tray of crunchy bite-size vegetables like baby carrots, cherry tomatoes, broccoli flowerets and celery sticks is always welcome.

## Traditional Party Mix

*Sonja Gaither*
*Macon, IL*

*I remember this recipe when I was a child at my grandparents' house in the 1970s into the 1980s. Grandma always made a double batch, then divided it...half for Thanksgiving and the other half for Christmas.*

2 c. bite-size crispy wheat
   cereal squares
2 c. bite-size crispy rice
   cereal squares
2 c. bite-size crispy corn
   cereal squares
2 c. doughnut-shaped oat cereal
1 c. pretzel sticks

1 c. garlic-flavored bagel chips
1 c. mixed nuts
2 T. butter, melted
2 T. Worcestershire sauce
1-1/2 t. seasoning salt
3/4 t. garlic powder
1/2 t. onion powder

Combine cereals, pretzels, bagel chips and nuts in a large roasting pan; toss to mix and set aside. In a small bowl, stir together remaining ingredients; spoon over cereal mixture and toss to coat evenly. Bake, uncovered, at 250 degrees for one hour and 15 minutes, stirring every 15 minutes. Spread on paper towels to cool. Store in an airtight container. Makes 22 servings.

Serve party snack mix or popcorn in a big bowl along with a scoop. A stack of lunch-size paper bags nearby will make it easy for everyone to help themselves.

# Festive Open House Appetizers

## 3-Cheese Smoked Almond Logs

*Vickie*
*Gooseberry Patch*

*A tasty addition to a cheese tray, alongside dried fruit and your favorite snack crackers. Smoked almonds come in several interesting flavors now...I may try wasabi soon, although Grandma would be very surprised by its hot flavor!*

16-oz. pkg. shredded sharp
    Cheddar cheese
2 3-oz. pkgs. cream cheese,
    softened
3-oz. pkg. crumbled blue cheese
2 T. green onions, finely chopped

1 T. Worcestershire sauce
1 t. hot pepper sauce
1 c. smoked almonds, finely
    chopped
1 T. fresh rosemary, finely
    chopped

Combine all cheeses in a food processor. Process, using the pulse button, until well blended. Add onions and sauces; process just until blended. Divide cheese mixture into 3 parts; form each part into a 6-inch log. Combine almonds and rosemary in a shallow dish; roll cheese logs in almond mixture. Wrap logs individually in plastic wrap. Refrigerate about 2 hours, until firm. Serves 30.

Fill an apothecary jar with Grandma's favorite old-fashioned ribbon candy... pretty to look at and sweet to sample!

# Grandma's Best
# Christmas
## RECIPES

## Shrimp Party Spread

*Jennifer Zacher*
*Ontario, Canada*

*I got this yummy recipe from a relative and it's always a big hit at parties. We've been making it for special occasions for over 30 years. Red peppers and green onions make it extra festive for Christmas. I make it one to three days in advance of the party.*

1/2 c. plus 2 T. canned
   tomato soup
8-oz. pkg. cream cheese,
   softened and cubed
1 env. unflavored gelatine
1/4 c. boiling water
2  4-oz. cans medium shrimp,
   drained and finely chopped

1/4 c. celery, minced
1/4 c. green or red pepper,
   minced
1/4 c. green onions, minced
1/4 c. mayonnaise
vegetable-flavored crackers

Heat soup in a small saucepan over medium heat until warmed. Add cream cheese; beat with a whisk until smooth. Dissolve gelatin in boiling water; add soup mixture. Add remaining ingredients except crackers and stir well. Spoon mixture into a bowl lined with plastic wrap. Cover and chill overnight, or until firm. Serve with vegetable crackers. Makes 12 servings.

For your appetizer buffet, give baskets a holiday touch.
Simply line them with colorful red plaid napkins. Fill with
crackers and chips for dipping...ready in a jiffy!

# Festive Open House Appetizers

## Gramma's Crab Filling

*Joyce Parr*
*Moscow, ID*

*My grandmother made this special recipe when entertaining the ladies' afternoon tea group. It's delicious on toasted baguettes... tasty for stuffing mushrooms or spooning into pita pockets, too.*

2 loaves bread, crumbled
1 lb. crabmeat, drained
    and flaked
4 eggs, hard-boiled, peeled
    and chopped

1-3/4 c. mayonnaise
4 green onions, sliced
salt and pepper to taste
toasted baguette slices

Combine all ingredients except baguette slices in a large bowl; mix well. Transfer to a lightly greased 2-quart casserole dish. Bake, uncovered, at 350 degrees for 10 minutes. To serve, spoon onto baguette slices. Serves 8.

Set out a wooden bowl of whole walnuts or pecans and a nutcracker for guests. It'll keep them busy while you put the finishing touches on party preparations.

## Cranberries Over Cheese

*Joyce Borrill*
*Utica, NY*

*A great appetizer, especially for the holidays. I usually have to make a double batch, as it goes quickly. A good make-ahead!*

1/2 c. sugar
1/2 c. brown sugar, packed
1 c. water
12-oz. pkg. fresh cranberries
2 to 3 T. prepared horseradish

1 T. Dijon mustard
8-oz. pkg. cream cheese,
  softened
assorted crackers

In a saucepan over medium-high heat, combine sugars and water; stir well and bring to a boil. Add cranberries and return to a boil. Reduce heat to medium-low and cook for 10 minutes, stirring occasionally. Add horseradish and mustard; stir well. Cover and chill. To serve, unwrap cream cheese and place on a serving plate; spoon cranberry mixture over cheese. Surround with crackers and serve. Makes 12 servings.

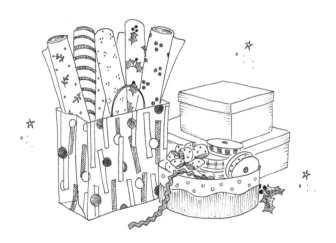

Host a gift wrapping party...invite guests to bring their gifts along with rolls of paper to share. Supply tape, tags, tissue paper, bows and other festive trimmings. Play cheerful holiday music and serve light refreshments...all the gifts will be wrapped in no time at all!

# Festive Open House Appetizers

## Sugared Pecans

Ann Farris
Biscoe, AR

*We have a pecan grove in our yard. The trees were planted by my
great-grandfather, grandfather and my daddy, many years ago.
These sugared pecans were a staple in our home.*

1/2 c. butter
2 egg whites
1 c. sugar

1/8 t. salt
5 c. pecan halves

Add butter to a 13"x9" baking pan; melt in 325-degree oven. Meanwhile,
in a large bowl, beat egg whites with an electric mixer on medium speed
until soft peaks form. Gradually add sugar and salt, beating until very
stiff peaks form. Fold in pecan halves. Spread mixture over melted butter
in pan. Bake, uncovered, at 325 degrees for 30 to 35 minutes, until
pecans are golden and all butter is absorbed, stirring every 10 minutes.
Cool pecans on wax paper; store in an airtight container. Makes 5 cups.

## Mrs. Claus's Cider

Jill Ball
Highland, UT

*What does Mrs. Claus do on Christmas Eve? She sits in her favorite
armchair in front of a cozy fire, sipping a mug of this cider.*

4 c. apple cider
2-inch cinnamon stick

4 whole cloves
Garnish: thinly sliced orange

Combine cider and spices in a saucepan over medium heat; bring to
a boil. Reduce heat to low and simmer for 10 minutes. The longer it
simmers, the stronger the flavor. Strain, discarding spices. Garnish
each mug with an orange slice. Make 4 to 6 servings.

Christmas is not in tinsel and lights...
it's lighting a fire inside the heart.
– Wilfred A. Peterson

# Grandma's Best *Christmas* RECIPES

## Papa's Party Hot Chicken Salad

*Edward Kielar*
*Whitehouse, OH*

*You'll have happy guests when you serve this yummy chicken salad.*
*We always serve this appetizer for holiday parties, and we*
*always have to make a second batch!*

3-lb. deli rotisserie chicken
1-1/2 c. celery, chopped
1/4 c. chopped onion
1 c. mayonnaise

10-3/4 oz. can cream of
   chicken soup
2 c. saltine crackers, crushed

Chop chicken, discarding skin and bones; add to a large bowl. Mix in celery, onion, mayonnaise and chicken soup. Spread mixture in a lightly greased 13"x9" baking pan; top with crushed crackers. Bake, uncovered, at 375 degrees for 30 minutes. Serves 6.

## Ham & Cheese Sliders

*Tina Matie*
*Alma, GA*

*These are a hit with my family, and very simple to make. They're*
*quick & easy for parties, or for a busy weeknight dinner served*
*with veggies on the side. Sometimes I'll add sliced turkey, too.*

12 small Hawaiian dinner rolls
2 to 4 T. butter, softened
   and divided
4 to 8 slices deli baked ham

4 to 6 slices provolone cheese
2 T. Dijon mustard, or to taste
Optional: sea salt to taste

Without separating the rolls, cut rolls in half horizontally with a bread knife. Place roll bottoms on a baking sheet; spread with one to 2 tablespoons butter. Arrange ham slices on roll bottoms; arrange cheese slices over ham. Spread mustard over cheese. Add roll tops; melt remaining butter and brush over rolls. Cover with aluminum foil; place on center oven rack. Bake at 350 degrees for 15 minutes. Remove foil; continue baking for 5 to 7 minutes. Sprinkle with a little salt, if desired. Serve immediately. Makes 12 sliders.

# Festive Open House Appetizers

## Cheese Spread on Crackers

*Leona Krivda*
*Belle Vernon, PA*

*This is one of my favorite go-to appetizers to serve. You can
prepare the spread and keep it on hand in the fridge.
When company comes to visit, you'll be ready!*

8-oz. pkg. shredded
   mozzarella cheese
8-oz. pkg. shredded
   Cheddar cheese
4-1/2 oz. can chopped black
   olives, drained, or to taste

4 to 6 green onions, finely
   chopped
1-1/2 c. mayonnaise
12-1/2 oz. pkg. shredded wheat
   crackers

In a large bowl, combine all ingredients except crackers; mix well. Cover
and refrigerate until chilled. To serve, let stand for 15 to 30 minutes at
room temperature. Top each cracker with a spoonful of cheese spread;
arrange on a baking sheet. Bake, uncovered, at 250 degrees for 15 to
20 minutes, until cheese melts. Makes about 4 to 5 dozen.

Wire woolly mittens of all colors onto a fresh evergreen
wreath...sweet little kid-size mittens will bring back
memories of Christmas past.

## Spinach Balls

*Mariann Raftery*
*Scarsdale, NY*

*Kids love these tasty spinach balls...they don't even realize it's spinach! This is a great recipe for making in advance.*

3 9-oz. pkgs. frozen chopped
  spinach
6 eggs, beaten
3 c. herb-seasoned stuffing
1/2 to 3/4 c. grated Parmesan-
  Romano cheese

1 onion, diced
1/2 c. butter, melted
1/2 c. margarine, melted
3 to 4 cloves garlic, minced
salt and pepper to taste

Cook frozen spinach according to package directions; drain well and transfer to a large bowl. Add remaining ingredients; mix together well. Cover and refrigerate for 2 hours or overnight. Remove spinach mixture from refrigerator; roll into 2-inch balls and place on ungreased baking sheets. Bake, uncovered, at 325 degrees for 20 to 25 minutes, until lightly browned in spots. Remove from oven and serve immediately. If using at a later date, cool completely after baking; freeze in a plastic freezer bag. Makes 8 servings.

Turn thrift-store holiday teacups into twinkly candles...just fill with pine-scented wax chips and tuck in a wick. Group them together on a mirrored tray for extra sparkle.

# Festive Open House Appetizers

## Hot Taco Dip

*Linda Peterson
Mason, MI*

*We make this delicious dip to enjoy every Christmas night, when we celebrate our family Christmas. Serve with tortilla chips.*

1 lb. ground beef
1 onion, diced
15-oz. can tomato sauce
4-oz. can diced green chiles

2 jalapeño peppers, finely
   chopped
16-oz. pkg. pasteurized process
   cheese, cubed

In a large skillet over medium heat, brown beef with onion; drain. Blend in remaining ingredients; cook over low heat until cheese is melted. Serves 6 to 8.

## Hawaiian Chicken Dip

*Shirley Olney
Moberly, MO*

*This was a recipe that my cousin has shared with me that she received from her grandma. I usually double everything so there's plenty for everyone to enjoy...they all love it!*

16-oz. loaf Hawaiian bread
2 6 oz. cans chicken, drained
1 c. sour cream

1 c. mayonnaise
1-oz. pkg. ranch salad
   dressing mix

Cut off top of loaf and pull out bread to create a bread bowl. Cube pulled-out bread and set aside. In a bowl, shred chicken with a fork. Add remaining ingredients and mix well. Spoon into bread bowl; serve with reserved bread cubes. Makes 10 to 12 servings.

My idea of Christmas, whether old-fashioned or modern,
is very simple: loving others.
—Bob Hope

## Sugar & Spice Nuts

*Leona Krivda*
*Belle Vernon, PA*

*This is a recipe I make to bag up and give as little gifts. I always like to hand people a take-home gift when they leave. A small bag with a pretty bow makes a nice little something for them to take home.*

1/4 c. brown sugar, packed
1/2 t. cinnamon
1/4 t. cayenne pepper
1 egg white

1 c. whole cashews
1 c. whole pecans
1 c. whole walnuts

In a small bowl, mix together brown sugar and spices; set aside. In a large bowl, whisk egg white well. Add nuts to egg white; sprinkle with brown sugar mixture and toss to coat well. Spread on a greased large rimmed baking sheet in a single layer. Bake, uncovered, at 300 degrees for 18 to 20 minutes. Cool; store in an airtight container. Makes about 3 cups.

Need a gift for a special family? Give a board game or a couple of card games along with a tin filled with homemade goodies... it'll be much appreciated on the next snow day!

# Festive Open House Appetizers

## Mom's Ranch Cottage Cheese Dip

*Tiffany Jones*
*Batesville, AR*

*I remember my mom making this delicious dip when I was a little girl. I always loved having it at holidays and family gatherings. Although she has passed on, this recipe brings back those happy memories of her.*

16-oz. container low-fat
   cottage cheese
2 T. ranch salad dressing mix

1/2 c. mayonnaise
1/2 c. onion chopped
cut vegetables or snack chips

Combine all ingredients except vegetables or chips in a food processor; process until well blended. Spoon into a serving bowl; cover and chill for 30 minutes. Serve with your favorite vegetables or chips. Serves 6.

## Pepperoni Bread

*Joan Thamsen*
*Conway, SC*

*This easy recipe was given to me more than 35 years ago by a dear friend. It has been a family favorite at all of our family gatherings ever since.*

8-oz. tube refrigerated crescent
   rolls or crescent dough sheet

3-1/2 oz. pkg. sliced pepperoni
9 slices mozzarella cheese

Unroll crescent rolls or dough; press seams together, if using rolls. Arrange desired amount of pepperoni slices over dough, overlapping sides and leaving a 1/2-inch border around dough. Repeat with cheese slices. Roll from one long edge to form a log; press to seal ends. Place on an ungreased baking sheet. Bake at 375 degrees for 15 to 20 minutes, until golden. Let stand for several minutes; slice and serve. Makes 10 servings.

Be sure to have a stack of recipe cards with your favorite party recipes...they're sure to be requested!

# Grandma's Best *Christmas* RECIPES

## Grandpa Arnold's Punch

*Valerie Bryant*
*Riverview, FL*

*My Grandpa Arnold would make this recipe every Christmas in upstate New York...then he'd put it on the back porch, where it kept nice and cold. Makes a lot, but sure goes quickly...so good! Apple juice or cider is good in this punch also.*

128-oz. bottle red fruit punch
2  89-oz. bottles orange juice
64-oz. bottle grape juice
46-oz. bottle pineapple juice
1/2 c. lemon juice

8-oz. can pineapple chunks
2 oranges, sliced, or 11-oz. can
    mandarin oranges, drained
Optional: 2 bananas, sliced

In a very large pot or other container, combine all fruit juices; mix well. Add pineapple chunks with juice and remaining ingredients; mix well. Cover and chill; serve cold. Makes about 50 servings.

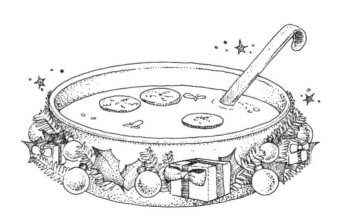

Nestle a sparkling punch bowl in the prettiest wreath.
Wrap mini gift boxes in scraps of gift wrap and hot-glue
them to a wreath form, then tuck in tiny, shiny
ornament balls between the boxes.

# Sweets from Grandma's Kitchen

# Grandma's Best Christmas RECIPES

## Gram Louise's Kolatchkies
*Paula Dejmek Woods*
*Frankfort, IL*

*Gram worked at a bakery and later married Grandpa, who owned the White House Bakery in Chicago. This is her delicious recipe that has been devoured for four generations now.*

1 c. butter
2 c. all-purpose flour
4 t. whipping cream
2-oz. pkg. cake yeast
1 t. sugar

1 t. salt
1 egg, beaten
14-oz. can almond, apricot or
   cherry filling
Garnish: powdered sugar

Combine butter and flour in a large bowl. Mix with a pastry blender or 2 knives until crumbly; set aside. Warm cream in a small saucepan over low heat. Add yeast, sugar and salt; stir until dissolved. Add egg; mix well and add to butter mixture. Stir until a dough forms. Cover with a tea towel; let dough rise for about 30 minutes. Turn dough out onto a floured surface; roll out to 1/4-inch thick. Cut into desired shapes with a small round cutter or other cookie cutters. Arrange cookies on ungreased baking sheets. Press the centers of cookies with your thumb; spoon in a small amount of filling. Bake at 425 degrees for 10 to 15 minutes, until golden. Let cool about 10 minutes; sprinkle with powdered sugar. Makes about 2-1/2 dozen.

A tiered cake stand looks inviting on a buffet and saves space too.
Fill alternate levels with bite-size goodies and Christmas greenery...
tuck in some shiny ornaments for holiday sparkle.

# Sweets from Grandma's Kitchen

## Mom's Drop Sugar Cookies

*Charlotte Smith*
*Huntingdon, PA*

*Great cookies! This recipe has been handed down for at least five generations. My grandma, my mother, my niece, my great-niece and I have all made and still make this recipe.*

1 c. butter, softened
1 c. sugar
1/3 c. milk
1 egg, beaten
1 t. vanilla extract
3-1/2 c. all-purpose flour
1 t. baking powder
1 t. baking soda

In a large bowl, blend butter and sugar well. Add milk, egg and vanilla; mix well and set aside. In another bowl, combine flour, baking powder and baking soda; mix well and add to butter mixture. Stir well. Drop dough by tablespoonfuls onto ungreased baking sheets. Bake at 375 degrees for 12 to 15 minutes, until golden. Makes 4 dozen.

On Christmas Eve, gather children together and snuggle in under quilts or in sleeping bags around the tree. Light some candles and turn on the tree lights...read *'Twas the Night Before Christmas* with a mug of cocoa to sip and a cookie to nibble. Memories in the making!

# Grandma's Best Christmas RECIPES

## Sugar-Crusted Meltaways

*Susan Kruspe*
*Hall, NY*

*My favorite cookie to add to a Christmas platter...the combination of orange and chocolate is so tasty! It's also a fancy-looking sweet for a tea party or other celebration. The baked cookies freeze well, so they can be prepared ahead of time for Christmas.*

1 T. orange zest
1/4 c. orange juice
3/4 c. butter, softened
1/4 c. sugar
1/8 t. salt
1 T. water
1 t. vanilla extract

1-3/4 c. all-purpose flour
6-oz. pkg. mini semi-sweet
  chocolate chips
Optional: 1 c. nuts, finely
  chopped
Garnish: additional sugar

Combine orange zest and juice in a shallow bowl; set aside. In a large bowl, blend butter, sugar, salt, water and vanilla. Stir in flour, chocolate chips and nuts, if using; mix well. Shape dough into one-inch balls; place on ungreased baking sheets, 2 inches apart. Bake at 325 degrees for 15 to 20 minutes, until firm to the touch. Remove cookies to a wire rack; cool completely. Strain orange juice mixture, discarding zest. Dip cookies into orange juice; let dry for 5 minutes. Roll in additional sugar; return to wire racks and allow to dry, forming a sugar shell on cookies. Makes 3 dozen.

Freshly grated citrus zest adds so much flavor to recipes, and it's easy to keep on hand. Whenever you use a fresh orange, lemon or lime, just grate the peel first. Zest can be kept frozen in an airtight container for up to 2 months.

# Sweets from Grandma's Kitchen

## Crisps Peanut Butter Cookies

*Linda Finfrock*
*Cary, NC*

*These cookies melt in your mouth! My neighbor Anna Neese made these cookies often and shared them with our family. She was like a grandmother to my two daughters...a special friend and great cook.*

| | |
|---|---|
| 1 c. shortening | 1 c. creamy or crunchy |
| 1 c. sugar |    peanut butter |
| 1 c. brown sugar, packed | 2 c. all-purpose flour |
| 1 t. vanilla extract | 2 t. baking soda |
| 2 eggs, beaten | 1 t. salt |

In a large bowl, blend together shortening, sugars and vanilla. Add beaten eggs and beat thoroughly; stir in peanut butter. In a separate bowl, combine flour, baking soda and salt; mix well and stir into shortening mixture. Drop dough by teaspoonfuls onto ungreased baking sheets. Press cookies with the back of a floured fork to make criss-cross designs. Bake at 350 degrees for about 10 minutes, until lightly golden. Cool on wire racks. Makes about 6 dozen.

Here's a simple trick to help cut-out cookies hold their shapes and bake up neatly. Place cookies on a parchment paper-lined baking sheet and pop into the fridge for 10 to 15 minutes, then bake.

## Christmas Pine Nut Cake

*Linda Walker*
*Erie, CO*

*My sister's husband talked fondly of this recipe. His mom made it for her family every Christmas. His dad would take the kids to the Colorado mountains to collect pine nuts for the cake. This is a true scratch cake, dense without being heavy. A slice is great with a cup of hot coffee or tea. These heirloom recipes are so important! I am pleased to share it, to honor my late brother-in-law and his mom.*

| | |
|---|---|
| 2 c. butter, softened | 1/2 t. almond extract |
| 2 c. sugar | 3-1/2 c. cake flour |
| 6 eggs, room temperature | 1-1/2 c. pine nuts, chopped |
| 1 t. vanilla extract | 1-1/2 c. golden raisins, chopped |

In a large bowl, beat butter and sugar with an electric mixer on medium speed until creamy. Add eggs, one at a time, beating after each addition. Beat in extracts. Beat in flour, a little at a time. Stir in nuts and raisins with a spoon until well mixed. Batter will be thick and heavy. Pour batter into a generously greased and floured Bundt® pan or tube pan; smooth the top of batter with a spoon. Pan will be full. Set pan in oven; set a pan of water on the oven rack under cake. Bake at 325 degrees for 1-1/2 to 1-3/4 hours, until cake tests done with a toothpick. Set pan on a wire rack; cool for about 30 minutes, until pan is cool enough to touch. Turn cake out onto rack; cool completely. Transfer to a cake plate; slice and serve. Makes 12 to 16 servings.

Cake flour is specially formulated to bake up light, tender cakes. If you're short on cake flour for a recipe, you can substitute one cup of all-purpose flour, minus 2 tablespoons, for each cup of cake flour needed.

# Sweets from Grandma's Kitchen

## Mom's Holiday Chocolate Pie *Kimberly Lottman*
*Big Island, VA*

*As far back as I can remember, my mom made this decadent chocolate pie twice every year, for Thanksgiving and again at Christmas. The rich chocolate filling makes it a stand-out above any other! I could eat it all year 'round, but like Mom, I save it to make the holidays special. Top with whipped topping or enjoy it just as it is, which is our personal favorite.*

9-inch pie crust, unbaked
2 c. sugar
3/4 c. all-purpose flour
3/4 c. baking cocoa
2 c. milk
5 egg yolks, beaten
1/4 c. butter
1 t. vanilla extract

Pierce pie crust with a fork; bake at 475 degrees for 8 to 10 minutes. Set aside to cool. Combine sugar, flour and cocoa in a large saucepan. Add milk; mix until well blended. Cook over medium heat until thickened, stirring often. Beat egg yolks in a small bowl. Add a small amount of hot milk mixture to egg yolks and mix well. Add egg yolks to hot milk mixture; simmer until thickened. Remove from heat. Add butter and vanilla; blend well. Spoon filling into pie crust. Cover and refrigerate until set; cut into wedges. Serves 6 to 8.

Baking together is a fun family activity and a great choice for kids just starting to learn how to cook. As you measure and mix together, be sure to share any stories about hand-me-down recipes...you'll be creating memories as well as sweet treats!

# *Grandma's Best* *Christmas* RECIPES

## Cranberry Christmas Cake

*Linda Vallaro*
*Warrenville, IL*

*I make this every year for our annual "Ugly Sweater/White Elephant Christmas Eve Brunch." It's always attended by 9 of my 11 children and 19 of my 26 grandchildren! It is a very enjoyable day with family and great food. My family enjoys eating this cake topped with homemade whipped cream...yum!*

3 eggs, room temperature
2 c. sugar
3/4 c. butter, softened
1 t. vanilla extract

2 c. all-purpose flour
12-oz. pkg. fresh or frozen
  cranberries

In a large bowl, beat eggs and sugar with an electric mixer on medium speed for 5 to 7 minutes, until slightly thickened, light in color and double in volume. Add butter and vanilla; beat for 2 minutes. Add flour; stir until just combined. Fold in cranberries; if using frozen berries, do not thaw. Spread batter in a buttered 13"x9" baking pan. Bake at 350 degrees for 40 to 50 minutes, until lightly golden and a toothpick comes out clean. Cool completely; cut into squares. Makes 12 servings.

Sparkly sanding sugar gives frosted cookies and cakes a pretty snow-dusted look. Sprinkle on while the frosting is still wet, wait 5 minutes, then gently shake off any excess.

# Sweets from Grandma's Kitchen

## Ginger Cake

Cynthia Scriver
Malone, NY

*This recipe was my father's mother's recipe from Canada. It was always made on a wood stove. We called it gingerbread.*

1-1/2 c. light molasses
1 egg, beaten
1/2 c. shortening
2-1/2 c. all-purpose flour

1 t. ground ginger
1/8 t. salt
1 t. baking soda
3/4 c. hot water

In a large bowl, stir together molasses, egg and shortening. Add flour, ginger and salt; mix well. Dissolve baking soda in hot water; add to batter and stir well. Pour batter into a greased 8"x8" baking pan. Bake at 375 degrees for 30 minutes, or until a knife tip comes out clean. Cut into squares. Makes 8 to 10 servings.

## Drop Cookies

Teri Austin
Yukon, OK

*This recipe has been in the family for at least five generations! It's a pretty basic cookie dough...I usually add chopped pecans to the dough and/or press a pecan half on top before baking. If not using pecans, you could add food coloring to the dough or sprinkle with colored sugar to make them more festive.*

3/4 c. shortening
1-1/2 c. sugar
1 T. vanilla extract
2 eggs, separated

4 c. all-purpose flour
4 t. baking powder
1/2 t. salt
3/4 c. milk

In a large bowl, blend shortening, sugar and vanilla until light and fluffy. Continue stirring while slowly adding well-beaten egg yolks; set aside. In another bowl, sift together flour, baking powder and salt. Add flour mixture alternately with milk to shortening mixture. Drop dough by teaspoonfuls onto greased baking sheets. Bake at 400 degrees for 12 to 15 minutes, until golden. Cool on wire racks. Store in an airtight container. Makes 6 dozen.

# Grandma's Best *Christmas* RECIPES

## Candy Cane Cookies

*Nancy Darnell*
*Coldwater, MS*

*This recipe was handed down to me from my mother. We made these cookies every Christmas, then my daughters continued the tradition. It isn't Christmas until we make the candy cane cookies!*

| | |
|---|---|
| 1/2 c. butter, softened | 1-1/2 t. almond extract |
| 1/2 c. regular or butter-flavored shortening | 1 t. vanilla extract |
| | 2-1/2 c. all-purpose flour |
| 1 c. powdered sugar | 1 t. salt |
| 1 egg, beaten | 1/2 t. red food coloring |

In a large bowl, combine butter, shortening, powdered sugar, egg and extracts; mix thoroughly. Blend in flour and salt. Divide dough into 2 parts and place each in a bowl; blend food coloring into one part. Make cookies one at a time. Roll one teaspoon plain dough into a smooth, even rope, about 5 inches long. Repeat with one teaspoon red dough. Place both ropes together, rolling dough back and forth together lightly; twist together. Place cookies on ungreased baking sheets; curve tops down to form the handle of canes. Bake at 375 degrees for 9 minutes, or until set and very lightly golden. Cool on wire racks. Makes 4 dozen.

Take the kids to a paint-your-own pottery shop. They'll love decorating a plate and mug especially for Santa's milk & cookies...you'll love making memories together.

# Sweets from Grandma's Kitchen

## Lillian's Spritz Cookies

*Peter Stadelman*
*Williamsville, NY*

*I showed my girlfriend my grandmother's recipes and asked her to pick one, and she chose this one. We made them and they were absolutely scrumptious! They're good any time of year...very special at Christmas.*

1-1/2 c. butter
1 c. sugar
1 egg, beaten

1 t. vanilla extract
1 t. almond extract
3 c. plus 1 T. all-purpose flour

In a large bowl, stir butter until softened. Add sugar, egg and extracts; mix well. Add flour; mix well. Press dough through a cookie press onto ungreased baking sheets. If dough is too soft, chill dough slightly before shaping. Bake at 350 degrees for 8 to 10 minutes, until very lightly golden. Makes 8 dozen.

## Cake Mix Cookies

*Kristy Lawrensen*
*Pierre, SD*

*Many years ago, I found this recipe in a vintage cookbook and added it to my list of cookies I make every Christmas. It's become my dad's favorite, so I always make sure to bring him an extra plate when I visit. I sometimes top the cookies with red and green sprinkles before baking to make them more festive.*

8-oz. pkg. cream cheese,
    softened
1/2 c. butter, softened
1/4 t. vanilla extract

1 egg, beaten
15-1/4 oz. pkg. yellow cake mix
1 c. powdered sugar

In a bowl, beat cream cheese and butter until well blended; stir in vanilla and egg. Add dry cake mix and stir until combined. Shape dough into one-inch balls; roll in powdered sugar to coat. Place on parchment paper-lined baking sheets, one inch apart. Bake at 375 degrees for 10 to 15 minutes, until set. Makes 2 dozen.

# Grandma's Best *Christmas* RECIPES

## Grandma G's Medallion Sugar Cookies

*Melissa Clemens*
*Mansfield, OH*

*My mother made these cookies every year...they were our family's Christmas cookies. She'd bake them and I'd decorate them, then we'd take a picture of the beautifully decorated, colorful cookies covering every square inch of counter space in our farmhouse kitchen. I have literally years of pictures of the cookies we made together. It isn't Christmas to me without her soft, sweet cookies.*

3-2/3 c. cake flour
2-1/2 c. baking powder
1/2 t. salt
2/3 c. butter
1-1/2 c. sugar

2 eggs
1 t. vanilla extract
4 t. milk
Garnish: candy sprinkles

Blend flour, baking powder and salt together in a large bowl; set aside. In a large bowl, beat butter and sugar with an electric mixer on medium speed until thoroughly blended. Add eggs, one at a time, beating after each addition. Stir in vanilla. Gradually add flour mixture to butter mixture, alternating with milk, until well blended. Cover and chill for about 20 minutes. On a floured surface, roll out dough about 1/8-inch thick. Cut out with cookie cutters into desired shapes; transfer to parchment paper-lined baking sheets. Bake at 400 degrees for 9 minutes, or until lightly golden around the edges. Cool on wire racks. Frost with Powdered Sugar Icing; decorate with sprinkles. Cookies store well in an airtight container; freeze well also. Makes 10 dozen.

### Powdered Sugar Icing:

2 c. powdered sugar
1/2 t. vanilla extract

2 T. milk

Whisk all ingredients into a smooth icing, adding more milk as needed.

# Sweets from Grandma's Kitchen

## Anna's Forgotten Meringue Cookies

*Diane Bertosa*
*Brunswick Hills, OH*

*This old-fashioned cookie recipe was given to me many years ago by a dear neighbor. It was always my son's favorite Christmas cookie.*

2 egg whites
1/2 t. cream of tartar
1/8 t. salt
3/4 c. sugar

1/2 t. vanilla extract
1-1/2 c. mini semi-sweet
    chocolate chips

Preheat oven to 375 degrees for 15 minutes. Meanwhile, in a large bowl, beat egg whites with an electric mixer on medium speed until frothy. Add cream of tartar and salt; continue beating on high speed until stiff peaks form. Add sugar, one tablespoon at a time, beating constantly. Beat until glossy. Stir in vanilla and chocolate chips with a spoon. Drop egg white mixture onto greased baking sheets by teaspoonfuls. Place in preheated oven; turn oven off. Leave cookies in oven for at least 5 hours, or overnight. Do not open oven for 5 hours. Makes 4 dozen.

A big glass apothecary jar makes a great cookie jar. Use a glass paint pen to add a personal message and hearts or swirls, just for fun. Fill with home-baked cookies for a gift that's sure to be appreciated.

# *Grandma's Best* *Christmas* RECIPES

## Edward's Apple Strudel

*Jackie Smulski*
*Lyons, IL*

*My dad served in the Armed Forces in the early 1950s. He was an assistant baker back in those days. This recipe was one of his favorite desserts that he prepared for holidays and special occasions. It brings back heartwarming memories of him. Note: If you can only find small 14"x9" sheets of phyllo dough, divide the apple mixture and make two strudels, each using five sheets dough.*

3 assorted apples like Granny Smith, Washington and Fuji, peeled, cored and chopped
1/2 c. golden raisins
1/4 c. soft bread crumbs, toasted
1/4 c. light brown sugar, loosely packed
1/4 c. walnuts, finely chopped
1/4 t. cinnamon
1/4 t. kosher salt
1 t. lemon juice
5 18"x14" sheets phyllo dough
5 to 6 T. butter, melted
1 t. white sugar
1 T. powdered sugar

In a large bowl, combine all ingredients except phyllo dough, butter, white and powdered sugar. Toss to coat evenly; set aside. Lay out one sheet of phyllo dough; brush with melted butter. Top with a second sheet of phyllo dough; brush with butter. Repeat layering with remaining dough and butter, creating a stack; a small amount of butter should be left over. Arrange apples over dough in a strip, about 1/3 up from bottom of dough rectangle, leaving 2 inches on either end. Lift the bottom of dough over apples; fold in sides. Continue to roll up dough with apples tightly. Place strudel, seam-side down, on a buttered baking sheet. Brush with remaining butter; sprinkle with white sugar. Bake at 450 degrees for about 15 minutes, until golden. Cool to room temperature; slice and sprinkle with powdered sugar. Serves 8 to 10.

Grandma often reached for her jar of cake spice, an old-fashioned mix of cinnamon, cloves, ginger, nutmeg and allspice. To make, combine one teaspoon of each spice in a jar. Use in baked goods that call for cinnamon.

# Sweets from Grandma's Kitchen

## Toffee Crunch Cake

*Leona Krivda*
*Belle Vernon, PA*

*A very yummy dessert...my family always looks forward to it!*

1 c. chopped walnuts, divided
1-1/2 c. vanilla wafer crumbs
1-1/2 c. light brown sugar,
   packed

1 c. butter, melted
15-1/4 oz. pkg. devil's food
   cake mix
2 c. whipping cream

In a bowl, combine 1/2 cup walnuts, vanilla wafer crumbs, brown sugar and butter; mix well. Divide among 4 greased and floured 9" round cake pans; press into the bottoms of pans. Set aside. Prepare cake mix according to package directions; divide batter evenly among pans. Bake according to package directions; cool for 20 minutes. Turn out layers onto wire racks; cool thoroughly. In a large bowl, beat whipping cream with an electric mixer on high speed until soft peaks form. Stack layers, dividing whipped cream among layers and on top. Sprinkle with remaining nuts; slice and serve. Makes 8 to 10 servings.

Whip up some old-fashioned snow ice cream! Beat one cup whipping cream until soft peaks form, then fold in 4 cups freshly fallen snow. Add sugar and vanilla to taste...enjoy!

## Frozen Peppermint Delight

*Gladys Kielar
Whitehouse, OH*

*A cool ice cream treat...perfect for Christmas in sunny places and in unseasonably warm temperatures! Drizzle with hot fudge and crushed peppermint pieces to make it special for the holidays. This dessert can be frozen up to one month.*

14-oz. pkg. chocolate sandwich
   cookies, crushed
1/2 c. butter, melted
1 gal. peppermint ice cream,
   slightly softened
12-oz. container frozen whipped
   topping, thawed

12-oz. jar hot fudge ice cream
   topping, warmed
Garnish: crushed peppermint
   candies

In a large bowl, combine cookie crumbs and butter. Mix well; press into an ungreased 13"x9" baking pan. Spread ice cream over crust. Spread whipped topping over ice cream. Cover and freeze until solid. Just before serving, drizzle with hot fudge topping; sprinkle with crushed peppermint candies. Cut into squares. Serves 12.

Dig into Mom's or Grandma's recipe box for that
extra special treat you remember...and then
bake some to share with the whole family.

# *Sweets from Grandma's Kitchen*

## Eggnog Pie

*Caroline Frazier*
*Dayton, TX*

*This is the easiest eggnog pie recipe. I whipped it up on a whim to have a dessert for our family gathering. I like to use a certain eggnog in a golden carton, but you can use any favorite. Feel free to use your own whipped cream, if you like.*

2 3.4-oz. pkgs. instant French
   vanilla pudding mix
3 c. dairy eggnog
10-inch graham cracker crust

8-oz. container non-dairy
   whipped topping, thawed
Garnish: nutmeg to taste

In a large bowl, whisk together dry pudding mix and eggnog. Spoon into crust. Cover and chill for 30 minutes, or until firm. Top with whipped topping and sprinkle lightly with nutmeg. Cover and chill until serving time; cut into wedges. Makes 8 servings.

A quick & easy sampler of goodies! Arrange ruffled paper candy cups in a vintage tin and fill each with a different treat. Try an assortment including fudge balls, sugar-coated nuts and bite-size cookies...yum!

185

# Grandma's Best *Christmas* RECIPES

## Jam Shortbread Cookies

*Jessica Delia*
*Preble, NY*

*My grandmother had 16 children and made everything from scratch. She was a wonderful cook and baker. These cookies are one of my favorites of hers.*

| | |
|---|---|
| 1 c. shortening | 2-2/3 c. all-purpose flour |
| 1/2 c. sugar | 2 t. cream of tartar |
| 1/2 c. brown sugar, packed | 1 t. baking soda |
| 2 egg yolks, beaten | 1/8 t. salt |
| 3 T. milk | 1/4 c. raspberry jam or other |
| 1 t. vanilla extract | fruit preserves |

In a large bowl, combine all ingredients except jam or preserves; mix thoroughly. Cover and chill for one hour. On a floured surface, roll out half of dough 1/8-inch thick. With a doughnut cutter, cut into circles with a hole in the center. Roll out remaining dough. Remove center ring from doughnut cutter; cut into whole circles. Spoon 1/2 teaspoon jam or preserves into the center of each whole circle; top with a circle with a hole. Pinch to seal edges; place on ungreased baking sheets. Bake at 350 degrees for 10 to 12 minutes, until golden. Makes 2 dozen.

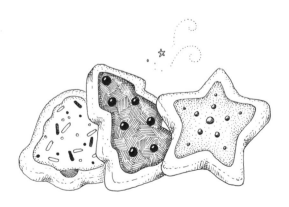

Best of all are the decorations the grandchildren have made...
fat little stars and rather crooked Santas,
shaped out of dough and baked in the oven.
−Gladys Taber

# Sweets from Grandma's Kitchen

## Granny's Orange Balls

*Pamela Stancil*
*Baileyton, AL*

*My granny used to make these no-bake treats every Christmas for her grandkids. She passed away in 2021 at the age of 103.*

16-oz. pkg. powdered sugar
11-oz. pkg. vanilla wafers,
    finely crushed
1/2 c. butter, softened

1 c. chopped pecans
6-oz. can frozen orange juice
    concentrate, thawed
Garnish: flaked coconut

In a large bowl, mix together all ingredients except garnish. Mix well, using your hands, if needed. Cover and chill until firm. Shape mixture into one-inch balls; roll in coconut and serve. Makes 2 to 3 dozen.

## Sugarplum Cookies

*Nancy Wise*
*Little Rock, AR*

*This is a sweet old-fashioned cookie recipe. My little grandson likes to help me make it. I pretend not to see him nibbling on the extra gumdrops!*

1 c. butter, softened
3/4 c. brown sugar, packed
2 c. all-purpose flour

1-1/2 c. small gumdrops,
    chopped and divided

In a large bowl, blend together butter and brown sugar; stir in flour. Fold in 1/2 cup gumdrops. Shape into one-inch balls; place on ungreased baking sheets, one inch apart. Flatten balls to 1/2-inch thick with the bottom of a glass tumbler dipped in sugar. Press several of remaining gumdrop pieces onto each ball. Bake at 350 degrees for 10 to 12 minutes, until edges are golden. Cool completely on a wire rack. Makes about 3 dozen.

Use kitchen shears to make short work of cutting up gumdrops, dates and other sticky cookie ingredients.

# Grandma's Best *Christmas* RECIPES

## Grandpa Joe's Potato Candy

*Jodi Clardy*
*Haslet, TX*

*As a child, I always looked forward to my Grandpa Joe making this candy every Christmas. Decades later, it is still one of my family's favorite treats. Every holiday season, my daughter and I turn on a Christmas movie and enjoy an afternoon of baking and cooking together in the kitchen. This recipe is always the first on our list!*

| | |
|---|---|
| 1 small potato, peeled | 1/2 t. vanilla extract |
| 6 to 8 c. powdered sugar, divided | 2/3 c. creamy peanut butter |

In a saucepan over high heat, cover potato with water; bring to a boil. Boil until very tender; drain. In a large bowl, mash potato until smooth. Add 4 cups powdered sugar; stir until blended. Stir in vanilla. Mix in enough of remaining powdered sugar, one cup at a time, to make mixture very thick like cookie dough. Sprinkle a sheet of wax paper with powdered sugar to prevent sticking. Transfer potato mixture to the wax paper; sprinkle potato mixture with more powdered sugar. Roll mixture out to 1/4-inch thick. Spread peanut butter evenly over mixture. Roll up tightly in the wax paper, starting on one long edge. Cut roll in half; wrap both halves and refrigerate for at least 30 minutes. Unwrap and cut into slices, one-inch thick. Cover and keep refrigerated until ready to serve. Makes 2 dozen.

Christmas is a time for sharing! Set aside a few cookies from each batch you bake. In no time at all, you can make up a platter of assorted cookies to drop off at a neighborhood firehouse, family shelter or retirement home.

# Sweets from Grandma's Kitchen

## Grandma's Favorite Chocolate Fudge

*Alisa Ricketts*
*Fairbury, IL*

*Grandma used to make this fudge during the holidays. She always said that the best time to make this was when it was cold outside with little humidity in the air. She wasn't fond of melting ingredients in the microwave; instead, she preferred the old-fashioned method of stovetop stirring. She said that this gave her and the grandchildren more time to visit. Grandma has been gone for quite some time now, but the memories will always be there.*

12-oz. pkg. semi-sweet
   chocolate chips
3 4-oz. pkgs. sweet baking
   chocolate, broken
16-oz. jar marshmallow creme

12-oz. can evaporated milk
2 T. butter
4-1/2 c. sugar
1/2 t. salt
2 c. chopped walnuts

Combine chocolate chips, baking chocolate and marshmallow creme in a large bowl; set aside. In a large heavy saucepan, combine evaporated milk, butter, sugar and salt. Bring to a boil over medium heat, stirring often. Reduce heat to medium-low; simmer for about 6 minutes. Pour hot milk mixture over chocolate chip mixture; beat well until chocolate melts. Fold in walnuts. Pour into a greased 8"x8" baking pan; let stand until hardened. Cut into squares. Makes 1-1/2 to 2 dozen pieces.

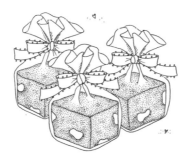

Mocha fudge is a coffee lover's delight. Simply stir in a heaping tablespoon of instant coffee granules along with the sugar. Heap individually wrapped squares in a brand-new coffee mug and give as a gift...clever!

## Grandma Phifer's Pound Cake
*Charlene Phifer*
*Denver, CO*

*This recipe is from my mother-in-law. It can be served any time of the year, but I like it at Christmas for family gatherings.*

1 c. margarine
1/2 c. shortening
3 c. sugar
1 t. lemon flavoring
1/2 t. vanilla extract
1/2 t. almond extract

5 eggs
3-1/2 c. all-purpose flour
1/2 t. baking powder
1/8 t. salt
1 c. milk

In a large bowl, beat together margarine, shortening and sugar with an electric mixer on medium speed. Add flavoring and extracts. Add eggs, one at a time, beating after each addition. Combine flour, baking powder and salt in a separate bowl; mix well. Beat flour mixture into margarine mixture alternately with milk. Pour batter into a greased and floured tube pan. Bake at 325 degrees for one hour and 20 minutes, or until a toothpick tests done. Cool in pan on a wire rack for several minutes; turn out onto a cake plate. Serves 12.

Make a delightful sauce in a jiffy to spoon over slices of pound cake or scoops of ice cream. Simply purée strawberry or apricot preserves with a few tablespoons of fruit juice...yummy!

# Sweets from Grandma's Kitchen

## Pecan Pudding Pie

*Sarah Gifford*
*Florence, AL*

*I found this recipe more than 30 years ago during a lunch break at work. It's a must to take to all family gatherings and sick friends. It's easy to make, easy to take and scrumptious!*

3-1/4 oz. pkg. cook & serve
   vanilla pudding mix
1 c. light corn syrup
3/4 c. evaporated milk

1 egg, lightly beaten
1 c. chopped pecans
9-inch pie crust, unbaked
Optional: whipped cream

In a large bowl, blend dry pudding mix and corn syrup. Add milk and egg; blend well. Fold in pecans; pour into unbaked pie crust. Bake at 375 degrees for 40 minutes. Cool for 3 hours. Cut into wedges. Top with whipped cream, if desired. Makes 8 servings.

Nothing says old-fashioned flavor like a dollop of real whipped cream on a slice of pie! In a chilled bowl, with chilled beaters, beat a cup of whipping cream on high speed until soft peaks form. Stir in 2 teaspoons sugar and 2 teaspoons vanilla extract...yummy!

# Grandma's Best *Christmas* RECIPES

## Cranberry-Orange Bundt Cake

*Annette Ceravolo*
*Hoover, AL*

*This recipe was handed down from my grandmother. I make this cake during the winter months, just like she did. Delicious cake...wonderful memories.*

3 c. all-purpose flour
1-1/2 t. baking soda
2/3 c. butter, room temperature
1-1/4 c. sugar
3 eggs, room temperature

1-1/2 t. orange zest
1-1/2 c. buttermilk, divided
1-1/2 c. fresh or frozen
   cranberries, finely chopped

Sift together flour and baking soda in a large bowl; set aside. In another large bowl, beat butter and sugar with an electric mixer on medium speed until creamy. Add eggs and orange zest; beat until light and fluffy. Sprinkle half of flour mixture over butter mixture; beat until blended. Beat in half of buttermilk. Repeat with remaining flour mixture and buttermilk, beating just until blended. Gently fold in cranberries. Pour batter into a greased and floured 10" Bundt® pan. Bake at 350 degrees for one hour, or until cake tests done with a toothpick. Cool in pan for 10 minutes; remove from pan and cool completely on a wire rack. Makes 24 servings.

Build a sweet gingerbread house and top it off with chocolate bar doors and shutters. Turn everyone's imagination loose with decorator frostings, assorted candies, even cereal and pretzels! Kids love this...just be sure to have extra candies on hand for nibbling.

# Sweets from Grandma's Kitchen

## Caramel Pudding Cake

Constance Smith
Lafayette, IN

*A recipe of my mother's and one of my very favorites for the holidays or any time of year. One year, my mother substituted this for my birthday cake...I loved it! I like this cake so much that I tend to double the recipe and use a 13"x9" baking pan or a 15"x10" jelly-roll pan. Perfect for carry-in dinners!*

1 c. all-purpose flour
1-1/2 t. baking powder
1/2 t. salt
1 c. sugar
1/2 c. milk

4 T. butter, melted and divided
Optional: 1/4 c. raisins,
    1/4 c. chopped nuts
1-3/4 c. water
2/3 c. brown sugar, packed

In a large bowl, mix together flour, baking powder, salt and sugar. Add milk and 2 tablespoons melted butter; beat for one minute. Fold in raisins and/or nuts, if desired. Pour batter into a greased 8"x8" baking pan; set aside. In a heavy saucepan, combine water, brown sugar and remaining butter. Simmer over medium heat for 5 minutes; spoon over batter in baking pan. Bake at 350 degrees for 40 to 45 minutes, until cake is firm and lightly golden. Serve warm or cooled. Makes 8 servings.

Any cookie or cake is even more delicious when drizzled with chocolate! Place 1/3 cup chocolate chips in a small plastic zipping bag and microwave for 45 to 60 seconds. Knead bag until chocolate is smooth, then snip off a tiny corner and squeeze. Try white chocolate chips for a different look.

## Cherry Drop Cookies

*Judy Phelan*
*Macomb, IL*

*My husband's niece always makes these yummy cookies at Christmas. They are made on the stovetop and are something you don't always see on a holiday cookie tray.*

1 c. butter
1 c. brown sugar, packed
8-oz. pkg. chopped dates
1 egg, beaten
4 c. sweetened flaked
   coconut, divided

1 T. vanilla extract
3 c. crispy rice cereal
1/2 c. maraschino cherries,
   drained and chopped

Melt butter in a skillet over medium heat; stir in brown sugar and dates. Remove from heat and stir in egg; return to stove. Cook over medium heat, stirring constantly, for 4 to 6 minutes, until mixture comes to a full boil. Boil, stirring constantly, for one minute. Remove from heat; stir in one cup coconut and remaining ingredients until moistened. Let stand for 10 minutes. Shape into rounded teaspoonfuls; roll in remaining coconut. Makes 5 dozen.

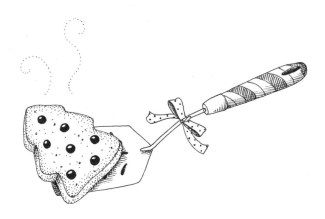

Whole pitted dates are often more flavorful than the pre-chopped variety. They're easily chopped with kitchen scissors.

# Sweets from Grandma's Kitchen

## Holiday Party Cookies

*Sarah Slaven*
*Strunk, KY*

*My mom used to make these cookies when I was little...*
*they were so special to me. Now I love making them*
*with my own kids, especially around Christmastime.*

1 c. shortening
1 c. brown sugar, packed
1/2 c. sugar
2 t. vanilla extract
2 eggs, beaten

2-1/4 c. all-purpose flour
1 t. baking soda
1 t. salt
1-1/2 c. candy-coated
    chocolates, divided

Blend shortening and sugars in a large bowl. Beat in vanilla and eggs; set aside. In another bowl, sift together flour, baking soda and salt. Add to shortening mixture, blending well. Stir in 1/2 cup candies. Drop dough onto ungreased baking sheets by teaspoonfuls. Decorate tops with remaining candies. Bake at 375 degrees for 10 minutes; some cracking may occur. Cool on wire racks. Makes 6 dozen.

Tuck a cookie into a cellophane bag and add a tag stamped, "Thanks for all you do!" Make up a batch to hand out to the mail carrier, the babysitter, the bus driver and all those other helpful folks we just don't remember to thank as often as we might.

# Grandma's Best *Christmas* RECIPES

## Orange Drop Cookies

*Lisa Hoch*
*Salem, OH*

*This is a recipe from my grandma's recipe box. It's something I have enjoyed baking with my family and sharing in Christmas cookie exchanges. These cookies are delicious, and so easy to make!*

1 c. milk
1 T. vinegar
1 c. butter, softened
2 c. sugar
2 eggs, beaten
2 t. baking powder

1 t. baking soda
zest of 2 oranges
1/2 c. orange juice
1/8 t. salt
5 c. all-purpose flour

Combine milk and vinegar in a cup; set aside for several minutes. Meanwhile, blend butter and sugar in a large bowl. Add eggs; mix thoroughly. Add baking powder and baking soda; mix completely. Add milk mixture, orange zest and juice, salt and flour; mix very well. Drop dough by teaspoonfuls onto lightly greased baking sheets. Bake at 375 degrees for 10 minutes, or until lightly golden. Cool completely; spread cookies with Orange Frosting. Makes 4 dozen.

## Orange Frosting:

16-oz. pkg. powdered sugar
1 t. butter, softened

1 t. orange zest
1 to 2 T. orange juice

Mix together powdered sugar, butter and orange zest. Stir in enough orange juice to make a frosting consistency.

Soft cookies can be stored with layers of wax paper between them to keep them from sticking together.

# Sweets from Grandma's Kitchen

## Old-Fashioned Brownies

*Sandra Mirando*
*Depew, NY*

*I searched a long time for a brownie recipe that had the chocolaty taste I remembered from childhood. This is it! Once you've tried it, you will never use a brownie mix again.*

1 c. butter
6-oz. pkg. unsweetened baking
   chocolate, chopped
2 c. sugar
4 eggs, beaten

2 t. vanilla extract
1-1/3 c. all-purpose flour
1 t. baking powder
1/2 t. salt
1 c. chopped walnuts, toasted

In a large microwave-safe bowl, microwave butter and chocolate together, stirring often, until melted. Let mixture cool slightly. In another bowl, whisk together sugar, eggs and vanilla until light and fluffy; add to chocolate mixture and stir well. Add flour, baking powder and salt; stir just until blended. Fold in walnuts. Pour batter into a greased 13"x9" baking pan. Bake at 350 degrees for 22 to 27 minutes, rotating pan halfway through baking, until a toothpick comes out with just a few moist crumbs. Set pan on a wire rack; cool completely, about 2 hours. Cut into squares. Makes 1-1/2 to 2 dozen.

For perfectly cut brownies, use a plastic knife for
a clean cut every time! Between cuts, wipe the knife
clean with a damp cloth.

# *Grandma's Best* *Christmas* RECIPES

## Grandma Tinius's No-Bake Fruitcake

*Linda Shively*
*Hopkinsville, KY*

*This fruitcake is one of my favorite Christmas treats. My grandma made it every year. She passed away more than 60 years ago. I was pleasantly surprised when my mother-in-law shared some recipes with me after I married her son, and the very same recipe was one of her favorites, too...small world! In Grandma's very old recipe, the fruitcake mixture was packed into the empty graham cracker box...a very creative way to re-use it! But you can use a baking pan.*

15-oz. pkg. graham crackers, finely crushed fine
2  14-oz. cans sweetened condensed milk
16-oz. pkg. seedless raisins
16-oz. pkg. chopped nuts
16-oz. pkg. candied cherries, halved if desired
7-oz. pkg. shredded coconut

Line a 13"x9" baking pan with wax paper or coat with non-stick vegetable spray; set aside. In a very large bowl, combine all ingredients; use your hands to mix well. Pack mixture firmly into pan. Wrap tightly with plastic wrap. Refrigerate for 2 to 3 weeks before slicing. Makes 24 servings.

Update Grandma's dessert spread with a Christmas dessert charcuterie board. On a large tray, arrange small portions of fruitcake, mini cookies and candies. Add a bowl or 2 of creamy frosting for dipping, some unshelled nuts and fresh or candied fruit. Fun at parties!

# Sweets from Grandma's Kitchen

## Fruit Cocktail Cake

*Sharon Laney*
*Maryville, TN*

*This recipe was given to me by my best friend from junior high school. Unfortunately, she left us way too soon. I make this every Christmas in her memory as I smile, remembering all the fun and crazy things we did together. It's a simple, old-fashioned cake, and I think simple and old-fashioned are good. So moist and delicious...my favorite "fruitcake." For Christmas, I double the recipe and decorate it with red and green maraschino cherries after it cools.*

1 c. all-purpose flour
1 c. sugar
1/2 t. baking soda
1 t. salt
15-oz. can fruit cocktail in
    heavy syrup

1 egg, beaten
1/2 c. brown sugar, packed
1/2 c. chopped walnuts
Garnish: whipped cream

In a bowl, combine flour, sugar, baking soda and salt; mix well. Add undrained fruit cocktail and egg; stir well. Pour batter into a greased 8"x8" baking pan. Combine brown sugar and walnuts in a bowl; sprinkle over batter. Bake at 350 degrees for 45 minutes. Cool; cut into squares. Serve topped with whipped cream. Serves 9.

A snowy winter afternoon is the perfect time to browse seed and plant catalogs and start planning your flower and vegetable gardens for spring. Snuggle up in a favorite comfy chair with a cup of hot tea while you daydream about warmer days to come.

# Grandma's Best *Christmas* RECIPES

## Easy Pear Cobbler

*Jennie Gist*
*Gooseberry Patch*

*We love this fruit dessert at Christmastime...it's a little different from the other desserts we enjoy!*

3 T. butter, melted and divided
6 very ripe Bartlett or Anjou
    pears, peeled, cored,
    and halved
1 c. all-purpose flour
1 c. sugar, divided
1 t. baking powder

1/2 t. salt
1/4 c. milk
1/4 c. apple juice
1 t. vanilla extract
2 T. brown sugar, packed
2 t. lemon zest

Spread 1-1/2 tablespoons melted butter in a 13"x9" baking pan. Arrange pear halves in pan in 3 rows, cut-side down; set aside. In a small bowl, combine flour, 1/2 cup sugar, baking powder and salt. Add remaining butter, milk, apple juice and vanilla; stir until well mixed. Spoon batter around pear halves. In a small bowl, combine remaining sugar, brown sugar and lemon zest; sprinkle over pears. Bake, uncovered, at 400 degrees for 30 minutes, or until bubbly. Serves 9.

On the third day of Christmas my true love sent to me
Three French hens,
Two turtle doves,
And a partridge in a pear tree.
  –Traditional song

# Sweets from Grandma's Kitchen

## Grandma's Pecan Pie

*Pam Hooley*
*LaGrange, IN*

*I am not sure why this pecan pie recipe is so different than others, but people rave over it and ask for the recipe. It is so very easy, and it is not so rich like some pies. My Grandma Ramer used this recipe for many years. We had a Ramer family cookbook printed, so many of her good old standbys are still available to all of us even though she passed away many years ago.*

| | |
|---|---|
| 1/4 c. butter | 1/8 t. salt |
| 1/2 c. sugar | 1 c. pecan halves |
| 3 eggs, beaten | 9-inch pie crust, unbaked |
| 1 c. light corn syrup | |

In a large bowl, stir butter until softened. Add sugar; beat well. Add eggs; beat until fluffy. Add corn syrup and salt; beat well. Fold in pecans and spoon into unbaked pie crust. Bake at 350 degrees for 50 minutes. Cool completely; cut into wedges. Serves 6 to 8.

A sweet favor if children will be coming to your holiday party!
Fill a basket with little bags of "Reindeer Food" for kids to
sprinkle on the lawn on Christmas Eve. To make,
simply mix cereal rings with candy sprinkles.

## Angel Wings

*Donna Denkhaus*
*Fenton, MI*

*My husband's aunt made these scrumptious German cookies every Christmas. We have many great memories associated with them.*

14 egg yolks
1 whole egg
1/4 c. vinegar
1/2 c. sugar
1 t. vanilla extract

1/8 t. salt
3 c. all-purpose flour
oil for deep frying
Garnish: powdered sugar

Beat egg yolks and whole egg in a large bowl. Add vinegar, sugar, vanilla and salt; stir well. Gradually stir in flour. Roll out dough 1/4-inch thick on a floured surface. Cut dough into strips, about 3-inch by one-inch; cut a slit down the center of each strip. Fold one end into the slit and pull through. Heat several inches oil in a heavy saucepan over medium-high heat. Add cookies, a few at a time; cook until lightly tan on both sides. Drain on paper towels; sprinkle generously with powdered sugar. Makes 4 to 5 dozen.

Use a sugar shaker for dusting powdered sugar onto cookies and desserts warm from the oven.

# *Sweets from Grandma's Kitchen*

## PMS Cookies

*Dianne Gregory*
*Oklahoma City, OK*

*We made these sweet & salty treats at Christmas...they were always a hit and gone before you knew it. Fun to make and sooo good! Hope you like them. Can also use saltines or graham crackers, and can also use white chocolate.*

16-oz. pkg. round buttery
   crackers
32-oz. jar creamy peanut butter

7-oz. jar marshmallow creme
32-oz. pkg. chocolate candy
   coating

For each cookie, spread one cracker with peanut butter; spread marshmallow creme on another cracker. Sandwich both together. Arrange sandwich cookies on wax paper and allow to set, or put in freezer for 5 minutes to harden the cookies faster. Melt chocolate coating according to package instructions in a microwave or double boiler. Dip sandwich cookies into chocolate, covering both sides. Return to wax paper until hardened; store in an airtight container. Makes several dozen.

## Chess Squares

*Kay Marone*
*Des Moines, IA*

*Delicious and oh-so easy to make.*

15-1/4 oz. pkg. butter cake mix
1/2 c. butter, softened
4 eggs, divided

16-oz. pkg. powdered sugar
8-oz. pkg. cream cheese,
   softened

In a large bowl, combine dry cake mix, butter and one beaten egg; pat into the bottom of a greased 13"x9" baking pan. In another bowl, beat remaining eggs; blend in powdered sugar and cream cheese. Spread over crust mixture. Bake at 350 degrees for 35 to 40 minutes, until golden. Cool; cut into squares. Serves 12.

The perfect Christmas tree? All Christmas trees are perfect!
–Charles N. Barnard

# Grandma's Best *Christmas* RECIPES

## Cowboy Fudge

*Jenna Harmon*
*Dolores, CO*

*This recipe is very special to our family...it has been passed down through four generations. My grandma grew up during the Great Depression and learned to cook with very little. The key to serving this delicious fudge is to cut it into small squares, so there is more than enough of this sweet treat to share with loved ones. Grandma passed this fudge recipe down to my mom and aunt, then to myself and cousins, and now to our babies who are her great-grandchildren. The good Lord took Grandma Kennedy home back in 2019, but her memory lives on with her cowboy fudge and many other recipes.*

1 T. plus 1-1/2 t. butter, softened
   and divided
12-oz. can evaporated milk

2-1/2 c. sugar
1 c. creamy peanut butter
1 t. vanilla extract

Coat a 9"x9" baking pan with 1-1/2 teaspoons butter; set aside. In a large heavy saucepan, combine evaporated milk and sugar. Bring to a boil over medium heat, stirring constantly, about 10 to 15 minutes, until mixture starts to thicken and reaches the soft-ball stage, 234 to 243 degrees on a candy thermometer. Turn off heat; immediately stir in peanut butter, remaining butter and vanilla until smooth. Pour fudge into prepared pan. Allow to cool completely at room temperature; cut into one-inch squares. Store in a covered container. Makes 2 to 2-1/ 2 dozen pieces.

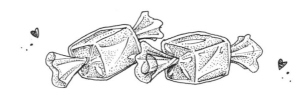

A candy-making hint from Grandma...a cold, sunny winter day is perfect weather for making candy. Don't try to make homemade candy on a rainy or humid day, as it may not set up properly.

# Magical
# Christmas
# Memories

## Christmas Dolls

*Darlene Runsten*
*Turlock, CA*

When I was growing up, my maternal grandmother lived with us. Her name was Sylvia, but we called her Namee. For Christmas, she always gave us practical gifts like slippers and pajamas...always something that we needed. I loved playing with baby dolls, and my parents always gave me a baby doll for Christmas. My mother and grandmother were superb seamstresses, so all of the clothes for my dolls were always homemade. One Christmas was really special because I received three dolls. One doll came from my parents...a "Betsy Wetsy" baby doll, complete with adorable clothes my mother had sewn. A second doll was delivered by UPS on Christmas Eve, from my maternal grandfather who lived in North Dakota. The package was huge! Inside was a three-foot "Miss America" doll, complete with a sparkly crown and a beautiful, shimmery white and silver pageant dress. Wow, it was stunning! I was ecstatic, to say the least. The third doll I unwrapped was a baby doll with numerous hand-sewn clothes from my grandmother, Namee. I played with all of the dolls, but of the three dolls, the one I cherished the most was the doll from my grandmother, because it was such an unexpected gift from her. Today, as I choose gifts for my family, I not only give the very important, practical, needed items as gifts, I also select special surprise gifts for them, as well. It is heartwarming to watch them open these surprise gifts selected just for them, just as I had been able to do as a little girl.

# Magical Christmas Memories

## Hiding the Pickle

*Marybeth Hunton*
*Centertown, MO*

While working at my first job after being married, I learned of the German Christmas tradition, hiding the pickle. My husband hides our pickle ornament somewhere on the Christmas tree. Over the years, it has become quite a competitive hunt for our three daughters and now their husbands too. We announce when they can come downstairs, and they come barreling down the stairs. Our daughters run to the tree; the guys walk behind them. The person finding the pickle receives ten dollars. We now do a separate hiding of a larger pickle for our grandchildren. The child who finds the pickle receives five dollars. My husband I are building a new house. Our oldest daughter's main concern is the Christmas tree will be on the main level...no more stairs to run down to find the pickle!

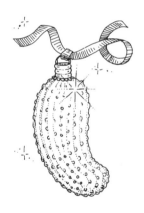

Christmas is the family time,
the good time of the year.
—Samuel Johnson

## Christmas in Arkansas

*Beckie Apple*
*Grannis, AR*

Growing up in the country holds so many special memories for me. I am well past my younger years now, but my memories of Christmas as a child will forever be young. We were not rich people, not financially that is, but rich in all that really mattered. My brother, sister and I knew we would each get three gifts from "Santa" each year on Christmas Eve. The waiting was so exciting! The joy of family, home and our Christmas tree is so vivid in my memory to this day. Nothing can ever compare to it. While I cannot return there physically, I can and do every year in my mind.

O Christmas tree, O Christmas tree,
How lovely are thy branches!
—Old German carol

# Magical
# Christmas Memories

## Jigsaw Puzzle Evenings

*Elaine Conway*
*Buffalo, NY*

When I was growing up, we lived in Buffalo, New York, where the winters are cold and the nights are long. We had a table in our living room that usually held a lamp and a few trinkets. Every winter, Mom would remove that lamp and set up a jigsaw puzzle that the two of us would work on. First, we would sort the puzzle pieces and find the edge pieces. Then we set up the puzzle, starting with the pieces that fit around the outside. Every chance we got, we would add a piece to our puzzle and watch as it became a picture. I still enjoy setting up a puzzle to work on through our long winter evenings!

## A Dollhouse Christmas

*Diane Himpelmann*
*Ringwood, IL*

One year when I was growing up, I wanted a dollhouse for Christmas. Coming home from Grandma's house on Christmas Eve, I couldn't wait to see if Santa had found our house. When I walked in the door, there were powdery footprints on our dark green carpeting, leading into our den. (The footprints were made by placing a socked foot in talcum powder.) There in the den stood a two-story dollhouse, ablaze with its own lights. I'll never forget it! Who says there isn't a Santa? There will always be that special Christmas.

# Grandma's Best Christmas RECIPES

## Christmas Eve Memories

*Jenny Maggio*
*Van Nuys, CA*

When I was a child, we had somewhat of a sparse Christmas. My brother and sister always tried their best to make the most of it for me. On Christmas Eve, my brother would do all his shopping for my sister and me. He would bring home a pitiful tree from my uncle's gas station, but we were excited to have it. We decorated it with whatever ornaments we could find. One tradition we had was to hang silver tinsel on the tree, one strand at a time, but of course my brother just tossed big clumps onto the tree. We would argue, then my sister and I tried to fix it up. Afterwards, we would go to midnight mass, and then go by my aunt's house to celebrate Christmas Eve. Our eyes would light up at all the gifts under the tree, and my aunt always made sure there was a gift for us. Being Italian, we would also have roasted chestnuts on Christmas Eve. I will always cherish the fond memories of how my brother and sister looked out for me, and made sure there were always a few gifts under the tree for me.

It is Christmas in the heart that
puts Christmas in the air.

– W.T. Ellis

# Magical Christmas Memories

## Baking Cookies with Grandmom

*Joanna Nicoline-Haughey*
*Berwyn, PA*

I will always cherish the memory of baking Christmas cookies with my grandmom. We would bake a variety of cookies...chocolate chip, pizzelles, coconut drops and many more. My favorites were the sugar cut-outs. Grandmom had a big tin of festive cookie cutters. We had such fun baking the sugar cookies, then decorating them with icing and sprinkles! She has been gone for many years, but never forgotten. I enjoy baking all these yummy cookies with my family in honor of Grandmom.

## Don't Open 'Til Dec. 24th!

*Betty Kozlowski*
*Newnan, GA*

I remember the year all of us siblings bought each other gifts. There were seven of us at the time, so our allowances were small, as were the gifts. Though there were no dollar stores at that time in the early 1960s, we did have the five & dime store! Underneath the Christmas tree cascaded the many tiny gifts, awaiting their opening. One day, as all but the youngest were out in the backyard raking leaves, our four-year-old sister's curiosity got the best of her. Later that day as I passed by the Christmas tree, I noticed each of the small gifts had been torn on top to see what was inside. What a surprise and chuckle it gave me!

# *Grandma's Best* *Christmas* RECIPES

## Christmas Morning Roll Skates

*Patty Hancock*
*Hawthorne, NJ*

I will never forget the Christmas that my four siblings and I all got roller skates. We lived in a six-family apartment building in the city, and we were living on the second floor. That Christmas, we all woke up in the middle of the night, full of excitement and anticipation, and convinced our parents to allow us to open our gifts from Santa. They hesitantly approved. We grew up poor, so getting the skates was such a thrill for us. I remember all of us putting on our roller skates and rolling around the apartment at four in the morning. I also remember the neighbors banging on the walls and ceilings because we were making so much noise! My parents had us all take off our skates and apologized to the neighbors. Afterwards, we all ran to our stockings and poured out all of our goodies, including the fuzz-covered hard candies at the bottom of our stockings. That is one Christmas I will never forget!

The children were nestled all snug in their beds,
while visions of sugarplums danced in their heads.
—Clement Moore

# Magical
# Christmas Memories

## Cookie Cutter Christmases

*Rita Munn*
*Manchester, TN*

My husband of many years and I are blessed with ten children and seven grandchildren. Christmas sometimes presented economic challenges for us, even early on. However, delicious homemade cookies nestled in decorative tins soon became the best Christmas surprise. I began collecting cookie tins and cookie cutters from the start. Our children each have a favorite tin and naturally a favorite cookie recipe. When we gather for the holidays, they know "their" cookies will be tucked into their special tin. By now, we have quite a collection of tins to be filled and enjoyed each Christmas. We have made a lot of sweet memories!

## Warmth of a Christmas Tree

*Jane Kueberth*
*LaVale, MD*

When I was young, my father would start by putting the big fat multi-color 1940s bulbs on our Scotch pine tree. I remember helping my mother trim the tree with our old glass ornaments. I was allowed to set up our creche beneath the Christmas tree. Then Mom would turn off all the lights in the living room, so the tree's lights were the only ones on in the room. I would lie under the tree and look at the creche, smelling the pine and soaking up the lights and the peace of Christmas. No matter how cold and dark it was outside, I always felt warm in the light's glow.

# Grandma's Best Christmas RECIPES

## Our Special Christmas Tree
*Brenda Montgomery*
*Lebanon, IN*

One year, I told my husband that he had to go get the Christmas tree, since I'd been doing it for years and it was now his turn. So he and our daughter went out and picked out a tree. The tree was tied to the car, and after they brought it in the house and he got it in the stand, he cut the rope. When that rope came off, half my living room disappeared! It was huge! So we moved a few things around and got it decorated. Even now, we still talk about our National Lampoon Christmas tree! That was one Christmas that the kids still remember and we still laugh about our tree.

## The Nonnie Box
*Sandy Coffey*
*Cincinnati, OH*

Here's how a sweet family tradition began. Ever since my mom passed away in 2012, we all began finding coins on the ground. They could be in any denomination. I have a box called the "Nonnie Box" for the coins, thinking of pennies from heaven, and that Nonnie put them there on the ground for us to find, They can be in our own home or in the car, etc. Actually, we mostly find dimes. On Christmas Eve, I count the coins. Whoever can guess the amount without going over gets the box and the coins. It's just a fun extra thing to do and then remember some of the great things Nonnie did for us.

# Magical Christmas Memories

## Grandma's Santa

*Sheri Kohl*
*Wentzville, MO*

My mom grew up with a great love for all things Santa Claus. She showered my girls with lots of Santa dolls, figurines and other toys when they were little. One year she gave us a Santa doll with a wiry body, which we placed on the chain to the kitchen light. The girls actually found his expression a little scary and were not fond of this decoration at all, but their grandma was so delighted when she saw it every year, that they kept mum about their feelings. It has taken on a whole new meaning, however, since my mother passed away a few years ago. Now we still put it in its usual place as a memory of their sweet grandma that we all treasure.

Not believe in Santa Claus?
You might as well not believe in fairies!
— Frances P. Church

# Grandma's Best *Christmas* RECIPES

## A Special Tree Skirt

*Glenda Tolbert*
*Moore, SC*

Years ago, I bought a green felt Christmas tree skirt at the dollar store. Every December, I would coat the grandkids' right hands with bright red acrylic paint and then press their handprints onto the skirt. After the paint dried, I would write their name and the year on the back of the tree skirt, under the handprint. Now I have years of sweet memories of my precious grandchildren.

## Dolls for Christmas

*Anita Gibson*
*Hudson, WI*

My mother came from Belgium, and all her family were still living in Belgium and in France. Every year, they would send me a doll from a different country. I started a doll collection with dolls from all over the world! My brother and I were small children and we remember getting that famous Christmas package from her sisters and brothers. My mom and most of her family are no longer here, but those beautiful dolls are with me in a display case. A few of those dolls have become worn through the years, but I cherish every one of them!

# Magical
# Christmas Memories

## Christmas at Grandma's House

*Sandy Perry*
*Fresno, CA*

When I was little, we always went to my mom's parents' home for Christmas. On Christmas Eve, we'd open our gifts. My cousin and I would always get a doll and an outfit that were nearly alike. I always got the blonde doll and a blue outfit, and she always got the brown hair doll and a red outfit. One Christmas they surprised us and gave us the opposite dolls and outfits. We were so happy to have a change! The next year they decided to go back to the original way. Whatever they gave us, we were always happy to have it and to have each other.

## Grandma's Manger

*Michelle Risoldi*
*Palm Coast, FL*

When I was little, I would stand on tiptoe to see Grandma's manger scene. She kept it on a sideboard in the formal dining room. If I stood really tall, I could just see over the edge and look at the baby Jesus. It never felt like Christmas until that little baby was placed in the manger...and I guess it wasn't!

# INDEX

## Appetizers

## Beverages

## Breads

## Breakfasts

# INDEX

# INDEX

# Find Gooseberry Patch
## wherever you are!

## www.gooseberrypatch.com

Email

Call us toll-free at 1·800·854·6673

# U.S. to Metric Recipe Equivalents

## Volume Measurements

| | |
|---|---|
| 1/4 teaspoon | 1 mL |
| 1/2 teaspoon | 2 mL |
| 1 teaspoon | 5 mL |
| 1 tablespoon = 3 teaspoons | 15 mL |
| 2 tablespoons = 1 fluid ounce | 30 mL |
| 1/4 cup | 60 mL |
| 1/3 cup | 75 mL |
| 1/2 cup = 4 fluid ounces | 125 mL |
| 1 cup = 8 fluid ounces | 250 mL |
| 2 cups = 1 pint =16 fluid ounces | 500 mL |
| 4 cups = 1 quart | 1 L |

## Weights

| | |
|---|---|
| 1 ounce | 30 g |
| 4 ounces | 120 g |
| 8 ounces | 225 g |
| 16 ounces = 1 pound | 450 g |

## Oven Temperatures

| | |
|---|---|
| 300° F | 150° C |
| 325° F | 160° C |
| 350° F | 180° C |
| 375° F | 190° C |
| 400° F | 200° C |
| 450° F | 230° C |

## Baking Pan Sizes

*Square*

| | |
|---|---|
| 8x8x2 inches | 2 L = 20x20x5 cm |
| 9x9x2 inches | 2.5 L = 23x23x5 cm |

*Rectangular*

| | |
|---|---|
| 13x9x2 inches | 3.5 L = 33x23x5 cm |

*Loaf*

| | |
|---|---|
| 9x5x3 inches | 2 L = 23x13x7 cm |

*Round*

| | |
|---|---|
| 8x1-1/2 inches | 1.2 L = 20x4 cm |
| 9x1-1/2 inches | 1.5 L = 23x4 cm |